CELEBRATE
YOUR BODY 2

THE ULTIMATE PUBERTY BOOK for PRETEEN and TEEN GIRLS

CELEBRATE YOUR BODY 2

DR. LISA KLEIN and DR. CARRIE LEFF
Illustrated by CAIT BRENNAN

ROCKRIDGE
PRESS

For general information on our other products and services or to obtain technical support, please contact our Customer Care Department within the United States at (866) 744-2665, or outside the United States at (510) 253-0500.

Rockridge Press publishes its books in a variety of electronic and print formats. Some content that appears in print may not be available in electronic books, and vice versa.

Interior and Cover Designer: Stephanie Sumulong
Art Manager: Janice Ackerman
Editor: Eliza Kirby
Production Editor: Erum Khan

Illustrations © Cait Brennan, 2019

ISBN: Print 978-1-64152-575-6 | eBook 978-1-64152-576-3

R0

To the ones that inspire and challenge us most:
Cameron, Brady, Reagan, Whitney, and Reese

CONTENTS

INTRODUCTION

| | | | | | | | | | | | | | | | | | | | | | | | | | | | |

WELCOME TO A BOOK ALL ABOUT YOUR
CHANGING BODY. While we know that not everyone
loves talking about puberty as much as we do, we are
here to help make this time of your life easier. You
probably have a lot of questions about what happens
to girls as they grow up and become women.

As doctors, and specifically as pediatricians (doctors
for kids), we are experts on the physical and emotional
changes you will experience as you enter your teen years.
We talk about puberty every single day in our office with
our patients. Not only are we doctors, but we are also
moms. We know your parents want you to have a helpful,
reliable source of information to read; we want this for
our own kids, too.

In 2015, we started our company Turning Teen to
help kids transition into puberty without shame and
embarrassment. We educate both parents and children
about the changes that happen during puberty. Our
workshops allow parents and children to learn together

about puberty, to help start the conversation about this special time of life.

Knowledge is power. If you understand what is happening to your body and why it's happening, then you will be more comfortable with the entire process. We know that understanding your body also means you will have more respect for your body and treat it in a wonderful way.

We firmly believe all girls are beautiful, strong, and confident. Being comfortable in your own body is important. You cannot be your best self if you are embarrassed about the body you live in.

We understand why you picked up this book. It's nice to have a way to learn about things like breasts and vaginas without having to talk about them at the school lunch table. You may have learned some information in your health class at school but still have a lot more questions. As your body changes, you will have new questions about what is happening. We hope you will use this book as a reliable reference to help answer your questions. We have also included a list of resources at the end of the book that are safe and trustworthy.

If a trusted adult has bought this book and handed it to you, then they have given you a wonderful gift. Hopefully, you can have open conversations with a trusted adult in your life about your body and your life changes as you grow up and mature.

In this book, we'll start by discussing the basics of puberty and how it's the beginning of a normal transition from being a girl to being a woman. You'll find detailed discussions of the physical changes you will experience, including breast development, pubic hair growth, and menstruation. We will also explain the changes going on in your brain, because you can better handle the emotional changes you will experience when you understand your brain. Finally, we will talk about sexuality and friendships. Relationships with your family and friends take on new roles and meanings as you go through puberty.

You can use this book in many ways. We would love for you to read it with an adult whom you know and trust, so they can help you with any questions that may come up. Sometimes even adults have a hard time talking about changing bodies, so we hope this book can help them too. Read it cover to cover or skip around to interesting chapters, and keep it around to use as a reference when you have a question or problem.

Welcome to puberty! This is an exciting time in your life. With the right information, you can enter this next phase with confidence, strength, and appreciation for your amazing body.

A NEW YOU!

· ·

This book is all about you and how your body is going to grow and change as you get older. You may be nervous (which is normal) or excited (also normal) about this change, but either way, knowing what to expect will make the whole process a lot less scary. Would you go into an audition or team practice totally unprepared? Probably not. So why would you want to go into puberty that way? Knowing about your body will give you confidence that it is doing exactly what it is supposed to do.

WHAT IS PUBERTY?

First of all, how do you say this awkward word? Let us break it down for you.

Puberty is a time when your body goes through changes on both the inside and the outside. Puberty may give you more things to learn about your body, but it also gives you more to love.

In simplest terms, puberty is a time when your body goes from looking like a kid's body to looking like an adult's body. Both boys and girls go through puberty. For girls, puberty can start as early as eight years old or as late as 12. Boys typically start puberty a little later than girls.

Just as people have different personalities, their bodies can be programmed to go through puberty at different times, too. Your older sister may start puberty after you, or your best friend may start changing years before you. And this is all NORMAL. The most important thing to remember is that puberty starts when your body decides it's the right time for you.

There will be a lot of changes during puberty that you can see happening when you look in the mirror. Your body will grow in all directions—up, down, and all around. You will grow taller and get a curvier shape. Another big change will be to your private parts (also known as your personal parts). You will develop hair in places where you didn't have it before (like your vulva, armpits, and legs). Your breasts will start to grow bigger. Your skin will even begin to change; it can get sweatier and oilier.

Puberty also causes changes to your body that you can't see in the mirror. Just as your body is growing and changing shape, so is your brain. You are becoming older and wiser, and the way you think will start to change. You may notice that you feel much more emotional than you did in the past. We like to say that in puberty you can feel like the whole emoji keyboard in just a few short minutes.

Is there a point to all of this? Yes! Going through puberty means your body will become capable of reproducing. It's actually preparing to be able to grow another human. The way your body prepares for this is through an important process called menstruation, or getting your period. Everybody has to go through puberty, because if we didn't, we would become extinct like the dinosaurs.

Puberty happens gradually over many years. You will not just wake up one day and magically transform from a kid into an adult. This makes the changes easier to get used to.

So let's learn together about this adventure called puberty. It may not be fun all the time, but being prepared means you can be ready for the changes that lie ahead. Let's get you ready for the journey of your remarkable body. Because here is the thing: **We get only one body—so let's love it, understand it, and take care of it.**

AN EXCITING TRANSITION

Life is full of transitions and changes. Can you remember how nervous you were on the first day of school? Or the first day on a new team? Change can make us nervous and scared, and that is totally normal. It also can be exciting if you are prepared for it and know what to expect. That's where this book comes in. The more you know, the more prepared you will be for your journey of change.

The period of time in your life when you are a teen is called adolescence, meaning "to grow up" in Latin. One of the main transitions in adolescence is saying goodbye to pieces of your childhood. Some days you will want more independence, and other days you will still want help from the adults in your life. Sometimes you will rely on your friends for guidance, and other times you will come running to your parents for hugs and support. This is all normal. It's a time of learning and adjusting to all of your body and brain changes. You are smart and capable—you got this!

Think about the life cycle of a butterfly. It goes through a lot of changes to transition from a caterpillar to a butterfly. It's an extraordinary process with an amazing end result—and that's exactly how it will be for you too. The caterpillar's transitional period happens while it's hiding in its chrysalis, but your transition happens while you are surrounded by others. You can call on your family and friends to help you embrace the changes you are experiencing. You will become a unique individual with your own style, personality, look, and talents. And as you gain independence during adolescence, one day you will be ready to fly on your own.

All the changes you are going through in puberty can be . . . well . . . overwhelming. But since you can't stop puberty (trust us, you wouldn't want to!), the best thing you can do is try to understand it. You were born with all the parts you need to travel on this amazing journey, and you have us, this book, and lots of people in your corner to help you become even more awesome than you already are.

What's Up with All These Changes?

Bottom line: At this time in your life, things are going to change—in a big way. What is responsible for all these changes?

Hormones are chemical messages that carry signals to different parts of your body. The main job of puberty hormones is to tell your body to start to change. Think of puberty as a movie with a great director and lots of actors.

	Cast of Characters	Role
Director	Hypothalamus and Pituitary Gland (small but important parts of your brain)	Directs hormones where to go and what to do
Star of the show	Estrogen	Makes breasts get bigger Grows hair in new places (armpit hair, pubic hair) Encourages healthy weight gain that leads to changes in body shape Helps ovaries and uterus prepare for menstruation and reproduction
Supporting star	Progesterone	Works hand in hand with estrogen to cause changes to breasts and uterus

Besides physical changes during puberty, there will be changes happening all around you. Here are a few examples of things that can change as you get older.

School

As you continue
advancing through school,
you will have changes
in your workload and
responsibilities. Each year
you have to get used to
new schedules, different
teachers, and, hopefully,
some great clubs,
activities, or teams.

Home

Your home should be a
safe and comfortable place. We hope that at home you
can feel free to be relaxed and be you. You may start
having more responsibilities and chores to do at home
as you get older.

Parents

Your relationship with your parents changes as you get
older. You want more independence and want to spend
more time with friends. They may want to hold on to
the times when you were younger. Your parents' job is

to set boundaries for you to stay safe. Having conflict with your parents is normal. Being able to work through these conflicts and find a middle ground is the goal.

Friends

One great thing about being a teen is that the friendships you make can last a lifetime. Surround yourself with friends who will be a good support system for you. Choose them wisely. Remember, your friends can influence you in good (or bad) ways. Start joining groups and activities that mesh with your personality and the things you like.

Emotions

You will start experiencing new emotions and will experiment with how to express those feelings. You may feel differently about your body as it begins to change, and that is very normal. Your brain keeps growing until age 25! Since parts of your brain are still figuring out how to work together, you are still learning a lot as a tween and teen.

Opinions

Your opinions will grow and change as you get older. You may discover things about the world that change how you feel about something you were once sure about. You may also see that in many situations there are no right or wrong answers, and that things are actually more complicated than they appear. This is a period of great development not only for your body but for your mind too.

It takes time for you (and your family) to adjust to all these changes. But this in-between time in your life is just the beginning of great things to come. You are paving your own road, and you don't know what lies ahead. This can be exciting and a little bit scary, all at the same time. It takes practice and patience to figure out what you want to be like in the future and how to become that awesome person you want to be.

It's All Normal

Attention, ladies! Remember . . .

PUBERTY IS NORMAL AND EVERY KID GOES THROUGH IT.

What is happening to you is natural and an important part of being healthy. It's important to remember that everyone's experience with puberty will be a little different. This means that your body changes at the time that is right for you—so your changes will not be the exact same as your friends'.

It's normal to feel different, look different, and be different than your siblings and classmates. Maybe you prefer long hairstyles, and your friend wears her hair short (and sprayed a different color every day of the week!). Or maybe you prefer English and history, but your bestie likes math and science. Your sibling might dress in sweats and gym shoes, while you are always dressed in the latest fashion trends. Learn to appreciate everyone's differences, including those from different family backgrounds and traditions than yours. There is so much to learn from everyone around you!

I can't think of any better representation of beauty than someone who is unafraid to be herself.

–EMMA STONE

SEX, GENDER, AND SEXUALITY

We think it's important here to pause for a minute and talk about the concepts of sex, gender, and sexuality, so we are all on the same page as we move forward. In general, a baby's sex (male or female) is assigned at birth based on the appearance of their genitals. Once a child's sex is determined, we normally assume the gender of the child: If there are female parts, that child is considered a girl, and if there are male parts, the child is considered a boy.

As a child gets older, they begin to have their own gender identity. Gender identity is your internal experience of your gender and how you feel about it. You can use pronouns to help describe how you identify; for example, "she" if you identify as a girl, "he" if you identify as a boy, or "they" if you do not identify with either category, or if you identify as both. If your gender identity is the same as your assigned sex at birth, this is called *cisgender*. If your gender identity differs from your assigned sex at birth, this is called *transgender*.

We can also describe people based on their gender expression; this is described as masculine or feminine and can apply to either sex. Gender expression is how you show the world your gender in your behavior, appearance, and mannerisms. For example, you may identify as a girl, but express yourself in a masculine way by preferring to wear short hair and a jacket and tie instead of dresses.

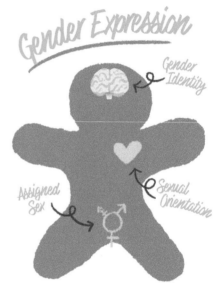

Gender Expression

Gender Identity

Sexual Orientation

Assigned Sex

It's important to understand that sex and gender are different from sexuality. Sexuality refers to who a person is physically and/or emotionally attracted to. The three most common terms that are used to describe sexual orientation are:

HOMOSEXUAL: attracted to people of the same sex (gay, lesbian)

HETEROSEXUAL: attracted to people of the opposite sex

BISEXUAL: attracted to people of either sex

You don't have to know exactly which category you fit into right now. It can be something that takes time to figure out, and it can change over your lifetime. It's important to accept yourself and others for whoever they want to be.

SELF-ESTEEM

Self-esteem is how you feel about yourself. Think about it as self-love, or how much you value your own worth. It affects how you think, feel, and act. Your self-esteem is affected by your relationships with others, but more important, by your relationship with yourself. Your appearance, or self-image, can influence your self-esteem. It's okay to admit this and work on being the best version of yourself.

It's human nature to compare yourself to others. Every person does this from time to time. When looking at others, especially on social media, you often see a highlight reel of their lives, not the entire movie with all the ups and downs. It's a common mistake to believe someone else's life is better than yours when you don't see the whole picture. Try not to let this affect your self-esteem. Challenge your brain to stop comparing, and get busy doing the work of being YOUR best self. One of our presidents, Theodore Roosevelt, said, "Comparison is the thief of joy." Imagine what he would have thought of today's social media!

Unrealistic expectations can lower your self-esteem. Everyone wants to live up to their potential, but it's important to recognize that, most often, you are your own worst critic.

How can you improve your self-esteem?

* ★ Believe in yourself.

* ★ Surround yourself with people who make you feel good, who are proud of you and build you up.

* ★ Don't set the bar too high.

* ★ Be kind to yourself when you make a mistake.

Do you have to like everything about yourself every minute of the day? Of course not! You will feel different in different situations and around different people. But you can always treat yourself with respect, regardless of how you feel in any one situation. It's hard work to be you, so appreciate yourself and learn to like yourself for your good qualities . . . and your bad ones. After all, there is only one of you!

SELF-CONFIDENCE

Self-esteem refers to how you feel about yourself; self-confidence refers to how you feel about your abilities. Because confidence is more about your talents than your thoughts, you can actually improve your confidence more easily than your self-esteem. **When your confidence improves, your self-esteem follows.**

Your body language and the way you speak shows off your confidence. You may even use them to pretend you have confidence when you don't really feel it inside. We don't expect you to feel confident all the time, but you can always look confident. Standing with your head held up, shoulders back, and chest out can actually make you seem more confident. Go ahead, try it! Having good posture (no slouching!) portrays an "I can do this" attitude. When seated, sit with your back straight and your feet on the floor. When you speak, avoid fidgeting with your hands, and make eye contact. Speaking in a positive, decisive tone (not a whisper) can make you sound confident and self-assured.

With all of the changes going on during puberty, it takes work to be confident through these transitions. The most important thing you will ever wear is your confidence. So if it's hiding in your closet, find it and put it on each morning. Stand in the mirror and rock your Wonder Woman stance. Practice having a confident conversation with yourself to see how you look and feel.

No one, no matter what they tell you, feels confident all the time. There are times when you will feel better about yourself, and times when you will question everything . . . and that is NORMAL! This is part of your unique journey, and you are just starting to build your path.

You have to work on your confidence. Accomplishing goals takes hard work, perseverance, and a belief that you have what it takes. If you stumble along the way, remind yourself that learning from mistakes builds confidence for the next try. Remember that you may have more self-confidence in one part of your life than another. For example, you can have more confidence as a soccer player than you do as an artist.

* COOL AND CONFIDENT *

Everybody wants to be more confident, but how can we really get there? Confidence is something that you gain over time through life experiences. It grows when you accomplish things that you never thought you could do. Remember the first time you worked hard on a school assignment and then you showed your teacher how well you knew the material? Or how about the time you practiced a skill (on an instrument, for a sport, or a step for a dance class) and then you mastered it? This is how you build confidence—bit by bit, slowly, over time.

WHAT TO EXPECT

There are many changes that happen during puberty. Remember, puberty is something that happens to you slowly. You will not just wake up one day with a totally new body. Because the changes are happening gradually, you have time to learn about them and slowly adjust.

There are three ways puberty happens for girls.

★ **Early birds.** These girls go through puberty first. They start around age eight. They may be the tallest in the class (just for a little while!) and will be the first ones to be the most physically developed among their peers. They may finish puberty before others have even started.

★ **In-betweeners.** These girls are not early and not late, but right in the middle between the early birds and the late bloomers.

★ **Late bloomers.** These girls don't start puberty until about age 12. They may wonder why their body isn't changing yet and why they look younger than their friends. Sometimes they will feel like puberty will never happen for them. Sit tight . . . your body will catch up!

It's important to know that everyone ends up at the same place in the end, whether they start early, late, or in between.

A Puberty Timeline

We want to lay out the puberty schedule for you so you know what to expect. Everyone feels better when they know what is coming. But while it's nice to have a timeline for what happens to MOST girls (read that again: we said MOST, not ALL girls), you have to remember that not everybody follows this order. Your body will do what is right for you, in the order that it decides.

What will happen first?

The most common first sign of puberty is something you cannot see, but something you can smell. It's called body odor, or B.O. As you grow up, you develop more active sweat glands, especially in your armpits. The more you sweat, the more you may smell. Body odor develops when sweat mixes with the normal bacteria (germs) on your skin. In chapter 2, we will teach you how to take care of your body so puberty doesn't make you smelly.

What is happening to my chest?

In most girls (about 85 percent, to be specific), the first sign of puberty that you can actually see is the development of breasts. It starts with something called a breast bud. Breast buds feel like small marbles or peanuts underneath the nipples on your chest. Over many months and years, your breasts will continue to grow and change shape.

Why am I growing all this hair?

Soon after breast development, you will notice hair in places that used to be bare! Pubic hair is hair that grows on your vulva. It's quite different than the hair on your head. Pubic hair is thicker, coarser, curlier, and often darker. You will start to get just a few strands, and slowly grow more and more hair until it grows out to your underwear creases and even toward your thighs. Hair will also start growing in your armpits. The hair on your legs will start to look thicker and darker. Everyone feels differently about these hairy changes, so we will discuss some options about hair care in chapter 2.

What is going on down there?

While all of this is happening on the outside of your body, changes are happening on the inside of your body that you can't see. You have an important organ in your body that sits under your belly button and above your pubic bone called your **uterus**. Only girls have a uterus. Your uterus has a very important function, and that is to become a home for a baby one day! On either side of your uterus are small grape-like structures called ovaries. Your ovaries are small but mighty and play an important role in puberty and reproduction.

Your ovaries and uterus work hand in hand to create one of the main events of puberty: menstruation. This is more commonly referred to as "getting your period." This process must happen for a woman to have the opportunity to become pregnant one day. During a sequence of events orchestrated by your star hormones, the uterus builds up a lining of blood inside itself. Then, once a month, for a period of about five days if you don't become pregnant, the blood leaves your uterus through your vagina. That's menstruation. (Read more about it in chapter 4.)

You may decide to have one baby, many babies, or none at all—that is up to you. This is not something you have to think about right now. But it is important to know that your body is designed to do this, if you choose.

Why don't my clothes fit me?

While your body is busy growing breasts and hair, it's also growing a lot taller. Before puberty, you grow about two inches per year. During puberty, your growth speeds up and you can grow two and a half inches to four inches in a year. This is like growing the length of a crayon in one year! Girls *usually* go through puberty before boys, so that's why some girls are taller and look older than boys during middle school.

While growing and changing, girls' bodies often become curvier. Not only do you develop curves on your chest (your breasts), but your hips and thighs can widen.

Your clothes may fit differently, and you will start to look more like an adult woman when you look in the mirror.

You are going to gain weight as you grow up, and this includes adding healthy body fat to your hips, breasts, and body. Fat gets a bad rap, but having enough fat is actually necessary for your body to function. **How much weight you gain on the scale is not as important as the health of your body.** Focusing on healthy eating and exercise is the best way to take care of your body.

YOUR BEAUTIFUL SELF

Most people think of beauty as something they can see and visualize. But really, it's much deeper than that. To be beautiful means to be yourself. Feeling beautiful on the inside will make your beauty shine on the outside. Sometimes you will feel beautiful when you do something courageous; other times it may be when you feel loved. Thinking positive thoughts and believing in yourself makes you confident and attractive.

Makeup and fancy clothes don't define beauty. The girls and women we see on TV and in magazines are not who you have to look like. Beauty comes in all different shapes and sizes. Bottom line: Everyone deserves to feel beautiful in their own way. Be your own kind of beautiful and shine from the inside out.

Your Body Knows What to Do

You should feel relieved that you don't have to know anything about puberty for it to happen; your body automatically does it all for you! Your body comes with a preprogrammed code that determines what you look like and a timeline for how you change as you grow up.

Knowing about puberty will help you feel better because you will know what to expect. But the time it takes your body to go through puberty is different for everyone. If you go through puberty quickly, your body may change dramatically over two years; if your body changes more slowly, puberty can take up to five years to complete. Sometimes your body will be changing slowly, and there will be other times when you notice more rapid changes. That is all normal. You will go through puberty at your own speed. The good news is that everyone ends up at the same place in the end.

TAKING CARE OF YOURSELF

. . . .

As you get older and your body changes, the way you take care of your body will change, too. Caring for your body in puberty is a sign of self-respect. It's a sign that you love your body enough to give it the attention it needs and deserves.

The way you care for your body is up to you! It's not something that your mom, dad, or best friend can do for you. Caring for your skin, hair, teeth, eyes, ears, hands, and feet are important in puberty. Here's what you need to know and do.

HAIR CARE

Your body is actually covered in hair. Some of it is noticeable, like the hair on your head, but you also have teeny tiny little hairs on your face, arms, and even your toes (go ahead, look!). As you go through puberty, your hair will go through changes too. You will start noticing hair in new places, including your armpits (called axillary hair) and on your vulva (called pubic hair). The hair on your legs will get darker and thicker. You will notice that your pubic hair has a different texture than the hair on your head—it's curlier and coarser, and may even be a different color.

On Your Head

Just as everyone's eyes are a bit different, everyone has a different type of hair. But no matter what, you will notice a change in your hair during puberty. The hair on your head may become more oily or greasy. This means it needs to be washed regularly. This will keep your hair looking healthy and smelling clean. Or the opposite can happen: Some hair types get very dry, and even your scalp can become dry, itchy, and flaky (this is called dandruff). In this situation, you may need to wash your hair only a few times a week.

There are lots of different hair care products to choose from. If your parent has similar hair to yours, they can help pick something that will work best for you. Sometimes, it's a bit of trial and error, so switch it up if you don't like your shampoo. Great products don't have to cost a ton of money, so shop wisely.

Should You Shave?

Some girls are comfortable with their new hair; others feel they want to do some extra grooming. Shaving is removing hair from your body. The most common places girls may choose to shave are their armpits and legs. Starting to shave is a decision you should make with the trusted adult who helps take care of you.

If you decide shaving is something you want to do, you have to be careful and understand how to shave properly and safely. Remember that using a razor blade to shave is like using knives on a stick. Razors are easy to use if you use them correctly, but you need instructions for your first time to do it safely.

Here are some rules for shaving:

* Always use a fresh, sharp razor because old, dull razors can cause skin irritation.

* Always use something to help the razor glide, like shaving cream, because it makes the job much easier.

* Never share razors with other people.

* Do not pass out, freak out, or flip out if you accidentally cut yourself and see blood. Little nicks are sometimes part of shaving. This is something you need to be prepared for. If this is too scary for you (and that's okay!), then you aren't ready to shave yet.

If this sounds like too much for you but you still want to remove some hair, electric razors are an easier, safer option that some girls prefer.

What About the Hair Down There?

Pubic hair that grows on your vulva takes a little getting used to. Initially, it will start off as just a few strands. Over time, it will get coarser and thicker, and eventually will begin to grow out toward the thighs.

Pubic hair has a purpose; it acts like a cushion to protect your skin and like a broom to keep bacteria and sweat away from your vulva. Shaving your pubic hair can cause itchiness and infections in a very sensitive area of your body. It is common to get ingrown hairs after shaving, which can become painful pimples.

It's okay to trim or groom your public hair so it doesn't stick out the sides of your bathing suit bottoms. You can use scissors or an electric razor to trim it shorter. Remember, it's your body, so it's your choice how it looks and feels!

SKIN CARE

Do you know your skin makes up about 15 percent of your body? Your skin is your largest organ. It's the first thing people see when they look at you. It's very important to understand how to take care of such a large part of your body. Your skin deserves your attention!

Your skin is like the peel on a banana or an apple. It's your outer layer of protection. You can tell just by looking if it's bruised or damaged. When choosing the perfect fruit to eat for lunch at the cafeteria, you probably reach for the one that has the fewest brown spots because you know it's the healthiest on the inside. That's a lot like your skin.

The most common concern tweens and teens have about their skin is developing pimples on their face. Here is why puberty can be a bumpy road. Your skin has a bunch of teeny tiny holes called pores. You also always have dirt or debris on your face that you can't see, as well as thousands of bacteria that live every day on your skin. As you go through puberty, your skin will start producing more oils. These oils combine with the dirt and bacteria that live on your face to clog your pores. Add on makeup or sunscreen and your pores get even more blocked and irritated.

When the pores get blocked, a bump—that is, a pimple—can form. Unfortunately, you cannot just erase a pimple off your face with an eraser (can one of you please grow up and invent that?!!). So the best way to prevent pimples is to wash your face and keep your skin clean. Washing nightly with gentle soap and water is the best way to start a simple skin care regimen. A daily oil-free moisturizer will help keep your skin hydrated and healthy.

When there are a lot of pimples on the face or body, it's called acne. Acne can be a hard thing to control for some teens. This does not mean you're doing a bad job of taking care of your skin; it just means you need some guidance. It can be hard to feel great about yourself if your skin is  angry. Talk to your parents and see what options are available to you at your local drugstore or pharmacy. If that is not effective, make time to talk to your doctor to discuss the different treatments for acne. There are lots of options for you.

Keeping your skin clean, well-moisturized, and well-rested (your skin repairs itself during sleep) can help with a lot of the skin changes you'll experience during puberty. Using safe skin products (the fewer chemicals the better) is the best choice for your young body, because your skin absorbs anything you put on it.

THE SUN AND SKIN

If you look closely at the skin color of the people around you, you will notice that everyone's is just a little bit different. Add that to the list of amazing things that make you unique! Melanin is the pigment in your skin that gives it its color. If you have small amounts of melanin, then you have lighter skin; if you have lots of melanin, then you have darker skin.

The rays from the sun damage the melanin in your skin and can lead to darker skin (tan) or red skin (sunburn); both of these reactions are damaging to your skin and can put you at risk for wrinkles and skin cancer. Wearing sunscreen every day and avoiding tanning beds and excessive sun exposure should be a regular part of your skin care routine.

SWEATY AND SMELLY

You will sweat more during puberty. Sweat mixes with the bacteria on your skin and can make you smelly! We don't want you to smell bad, so here are a few ways to avoid having body odor.

★ **Wash your body regularly.** Remember that body odor comes from a combination of sweat and bacteria on the surface of the skin. It's very important to wash your body every day, especially under your arms. This will help you smell clean.

- ★ **Use deodorant.** Deodorant helps deodorize your body, so it prevents and gets rid of any smell. Since what you put on your skin gets into your body, it's best to use a natural deodorant with fewer chemicals. Antiperspirants stop you from sweating. All antiperspirants are made from aluminum, which plugs up your sweat glands. We recommend buying natural deodorants without antiperspirants, because they are the safest for your changing body.

- ★ **Wear clean clothes.** Wearing your favorite shirt all the time can make it stinky. Show off your whole wardrobe and get your clothes washed between wears. Better yet, learn how to do laundry and help wash your clothes yourself!

TEETH

Your smile is one of the first things others notice about you, so dental care is important. The best way to take care of your teeth is to brush them with toothpaste twice a day. Find a toothpaste with fluoride to help prevent cavities. There are other positives to brushing besides a beautiful smile. Brushing helps remove food particles, bacteria, and plaque, getting rid of bad breath (who wants that?!). Flossing is an important habit as well because it cleans the hard-to-reach places between teeth.

What you eat and drink also affects your teeth. Sugary foods and drinks damage your tooth enamel, which protects your teeth. Water is the best thing to drink all day; it helps clean your teeth while you hydrate.

It's rare for your adult teeth to come in perfectly straight, so a lot of kids get braces. An orthodontist will decide what type of dental appliance you need, but braces are the most common. Use the bands on your braces as a chance to accessorize and show off your favorite colors or school spirit. Don't brush off your oral care. It will ensure that you will have a healthy smile you can be proud of as an adult.

> Your smile is your logo, your personality is your business card, how you leave others feeling after having an experience with you becomes your trademark.
>
> **–JAY DANZIE**

EYES

You want your eyes to be healthy so you can enjoy the amazing world around you. As you get older, you may notice your vision is changing. It's important to have your eyes checked yearly so you can read your books easily and see the board at school clearly.

Wearing glasses is a fabulous way to accessorize and show your personality. Neon pink or berry blue? You decide what looks best on you! You can also decide if you want to wear contact lenses as you get older. This is an added responsibility but can be done easily with help from your doctor and parents.

As the saying goes, "The eyes are the window to your soul." Your eyes can convey your emotions and tell a lot about you. Learning to make eye contact is an important part of getting older; this lets people know you are actively listening and interested in what they are saying.

COOL AND CONFIDENT

Your body language helps convey your level of confidence. Make eye contact when talking and listening to others. Staring at the floor, your phone, or off into space when having a conversation makes the person you are talking to think you are not interested. People have respect for those who have self-confidence and respect themselves and others.

EARS

Thanks to your ears, you can listen to music, hear your friend's funny stories, and get advice from your parents (like it or not!). Your ears are very sensitive and fragile on the inside. Your ear canal, eardrum, and the tiny bones behind your eardrum are all important for your hearing, and you need to protect them.

Never put anything in your ear canal—not even cotton swabs. This way you will not damage your eardrum, which could affect your hearing. A little bit of wax in your ears is not only normal, but it's also important to stop harmful particles from entering the canal. If you want to clean wax from your ear, take a washcloth and clean around the opening to your ear. If you have wax build-up, visit your doctor for a cleaning.

LISTEN SAFELY

Be careful around very loud sounds. Loud and frequent noise can damage your hearing. Millions of teenagers are at risk for hearing loss because of loud concerts and the unsafe use of headphones and earbuds. So enjoy your music—just turn down the volume!

HANDS AND FEET

You use your hands for so many different things: sensing temperature and texture, greeting people with a handshake, and doing things like brushing your teeth and using your phone. There are lots of bacteria on the surface of your skin, especially on your hands, from all these activities. Keeping your hands clean is one of the most important things you can do to stay healthy. So be sure to wash your hands after going to the bathroom and before you eat.

Painting your nails is a fun activity some girls like to do with friends or family members. You may have a special occasion and get treated to a manicure sometimes. If you get permission to go to a nail salon, make sure you ask for clean, sterilized manicure tools to avoid any infections.

Your feet are keeping busy: walking all over school, playing sports, dancing, and literally supporting you all day long. Be nice to your feet and wear supportive, protective shoes.

Cleaning your feet is important too because this is another place where odor can be an issue. It's worth the extra step in the shower to actually wash your feet with soap and water to help keep them smelling clean. Get help properly cutting your toenails to avoid ingrown toenails. Be sure to let your doctor know if you see any new bumps on your feet; sometimes people get warts that need treatment.

Your hands and feet are some of the most used parts of your body, so give them love and attention!

YOUR BEAUTIFUL BODY

• •

EVERYBODY is unique. EVERY BODY is unique. Your body is beautiful now, and it will be beautiful as it goes through puberty and comes out the other side.

It's easy to figure out what you don't like about your body. But can you challenge yourself to figure out your best qualities? Make a list of what you love about yourself. What makes you unique? It can be helpful to focus on what your body can do, rather than what it looks like. Do you pick your friends based on their hairstyle? We hope not. We want people to think about and appreciate you for who you are: as a person, a friend, a student. Focusing on your looks takes away from developing your important qualities.

No one feels great if they feel weighed down by their body or are eating food that is not nourishing. You won't feel as energetic if you are inactive, either; your body is meant to move. So establish good habits now. Eat healthy foods, move your body, and work hard at feeling good about yourself. Taking care of your body is a sign of self-respect.

YOUR GROWING BODY

Hopefully, you have been taking good care of your body before puberty, so you can continue your established good habits and pick up some new ones along the way. Let's walk through what you can expect from your growing body.

Up and Up

As a child, you grew about two to two and a half inches each year. During puberty, you can have growth spurts and grow three or more inches in a year. Since you grow only a tiny bit at a time, you will not necessarily notice that you have grown when you look in the mirror each day. But when you see someone who hasn't seen you in a long time, they may comment on how much taller you look. Girls have their largest growth spurt the year before they start menstruation. Once girls start their period, the pace of their growth slows. Most girls stop growing in height about two years after they start their period.

Sometimes during growth spurts, girls complain of growing pains, which are usually described as muscle aches or throbs in the legs at night. You can try massaging the sore areas and using a heating pad. If your pain is frequent or bothersome, be sure to discuss it with your doctor.

A common question girls ask us in the doctor's office is, "How tall am I going to be?" There are different ways to try to predict your adult height. One way is to look at how tall your parents are and calculate what doctors call the midparental height. This is generally accurate within about three inches. The formula is below, if you want to calculate it for yourself.

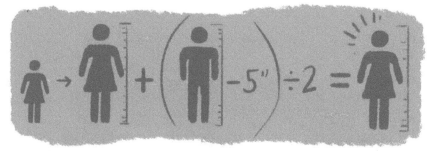

For girls: Your mom's height + (your dad's height - 5 inches) / 2 = future height

For boys: Your dad's height + (your mom's height + 5 inches) / 2 = future height

Another way you can try to predict your height is to look at the growth chart that your doctor has been keeping in your record. At your next appointment, ask your doctor to review the growth chart with you. Based on how much you have grown so far, you can estimate your final height.

What you should know is that your final height is not under your control, as this was programmed into your genes before you were even born! Your job is to keep your body healthy so it has enough energy to reach its full potential.

Building Strong Bones

What makes your bones strong? Calcium! Calcium is an important mineral that is critical for your body at this time of your life. Your bones are busy using a lot of calcium while they are growing longer and stronger. Plus, you actually strengthen your bones for life while you are a teen. You can give your body the building blocks to build strong bones by eating foods that are rich in calcium.

What are your calcium needs as a teen?

★ 1,300 milligrams per day

★ Four servings of calcium-rich foods per day

What foods can you eat that contain calcium?

★ Dairy (such as milk, cheese, yogurt)

★ Green leafy vegetables (such as broccoli, spinach, kale)

★ Almonds

★ Avocados

★ Salmon

★ Chickpeas

What if you can't eat that much calcium a day? Supplement with vitamins—but the best way to get your nutrients is always through your food.

When you go to your yearly checkup at the doctor, one of the many important things to do is check your spine. While your body is doing all this growth, you can develop scoliosis, or curvature of your spine. Girls get scoliosis more often than boys. Sometimes it straightens itself out over time, and sometimes special bone doctors need to help get you straightened out.

Here are a few things you can do to keep yourself healthy and your back straight.

* Wear your backpack with the straps on both shoulders.

* Strengthen your core muscles with exercises like sit-ups.

* Pay attention to your posture; stand with your shoulders back and chest out, and don't slouch when you sit. (This helps with confidence too.)

Your Changing Shape

An important part of puberty is the change in your body shape. You are going to change from looking like a child to looking more like an adult. You will not only be growing taller, but also putting on weight to support your body's changing functions. Gaining 15 to 30 pounds of muscle, bone, and fat during puberty is *expected*.

Body Mass Index (BMI) is a commonly used equation to help determine the right weight for your height. Doctors use this to help discuss how to prevent health problems related to excess weight gain. But remember that BMI and weight are only two of the many important factors that determine your overall health.

There is no ideal body weight, shape, or size. To a great extent, these things are predetermined in our DNA (our genetic code) before we are even born. Some girls like to know their ideal body weight. Doctors can look at growth charts and scientific formulas that tell us numbers. **But the right weight for your body is one at which you feel strong, energetic, and comfortable.**

As your body shape changes, you will notice your clothes will start to fit differently and you may change sizes frequently. Try not to get frustrated if your clothing doesn't fit the way it used to. Your shirts have to fit over your growing breasts, and your pants have to pull over your fuller hips and buttocks. We will be honest: It does take time to get used to your new, unfamiliar body. But hang in there—with healthy habits and time, you will get comfortable in this new body.

DEVELOPING BREASTS

Breasts are a part of your body that changes during puberty. It's important to remember that your body has a fantastic design, and every part has a purpose. Your breasts are growing to become capable of feeding a baby one day. That is pretty amazing!

Your breasts are made of up of two different types of tissue:

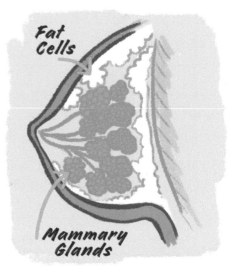

* Fat cells

* Mammary glands (the parts that produce milk)

In most girls (85 percent to be specific), the first sign of puberty that you can actually *see* is the development of breasts. Breast budding is the medical term used to describe the start of growing breasts (this has nothing to do with a flower!). Breast buds are bumps that feel like small marbles or peanuts underneath your nipples. The hormones your body produces during puberty (primarily estrogen) cause breast development.

The areola (the dark part around the nipple) grows larger and darker, and the nipple often changes, too. Your nipples may stick out and become raised and pointed, or they may lie flat or be inverted (go inward). Your breasts will change shape and sometimes seem pointy during development, and later on, may become more rounded. Over many months and years, your breasts will continue to grow and change size and shape.

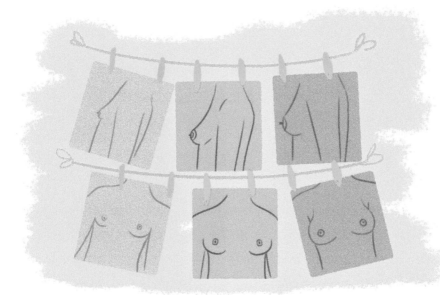

Just as we all have different hairstyles, we all have different breasts. No two breasts are exactly the same. Some are fuller, some are pointier, some stand up straight, and some hang low. Even your own two breasts may not be exactly the same; one side (usually the left) may be slightly bigger than the other.

In our culture, girls' breasts are considered private parts. And yet, there is a lot of attention paid to women's breasts. You may have noticed on TV, in movies, in video games, or even walking around the mall that some girls accentuate their breasts by wearing tight or revealing clothing. You may even hear of people who have surgery to make their breasts bigger.

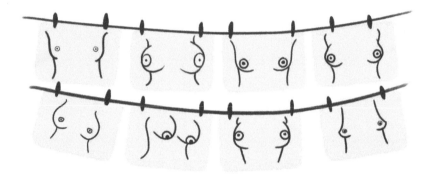

Breast size or shape does NOT determine anything except the size of your bra. The characteristics of your breasts are mostly determined by genetics, with some influence from body weight. Breast size is not something you have control over—and therefore you should not stress over it.

Again, thinking about function helps here; your breasts have the important ability to feed a baby one day. You may have mixed feelings about your breasts. Some days you may think that your growth is exciting, and other days you may be annoyed with your body changes, including your breasts. These are normal feelings as you adjust to your changing body.

COOL AND CONFIDENT

"WHAT OTHERS THINK OF ME IS **THEIR** CHOICE. WHAT I THINK OF ME IS **MY** CHOICE." Get busy being your best self. You can't become better if you are comparing yourself to others or tearing others down. No one is better at being you than you! Show the world who is inside of your fantastic body. Express yourself through activities—whether that's through music, being fierce on an athletic field, or showing off your creativity in art or fashion or writing. The person whose opinion about you matters the most is YOU.

Buying a Bra

When your breasts start to grow and change, you may decide that you want an extra layer to cover them and keep them protected. It's common for your breasts to be a little tender or sensitive while they are growing, and a bra may also help with that. But wearing an extra layer every day underneath your shirt can take some getting used to. A good strategy is to start by wearing a camisole or tank top underneath your shirt even before you need to wear a bra. You also want to keep your private parts private. Some shirts are made of a thin material and are see-through, so it's helpful to wear a layer underneath.

Girls with larger breasts may like the stability provided by a supportive bra. Your breasts are constantly changing, even as an adult, so you will need different types of bras for different stages of life.

There are so many different types of bras to choose from. It's helpful to touch and feel and look around at all your choices, so you know what kind of bra works for you. You may want to visit a store that sells women's underwear and try on several styles of bras. Or you may prefer to have a trusted adult buy a few different kinds at the store and then try them on in the comfort of your own home.

Bras come in all kinds of styles, colors, shapes, and sizes. Bras can be supportive and hold up breasts, and some are just for fashion or comfort or modesty. You may prefer one type of bra for a school day, and a different type for a fancy dress or a soccer practice. There is a bra for every size, shape, and event you are looking for.

BRAS: IT'S YOUR CHOICE!

Hook: Front hook, back hook, no hook

Cup Lining: Padded, lightly lined, no padding

Straps: Shoulder straps, crossing back straps, halter straps, no straps (strapless)

Material: Cotton, lace, satin, spandex

Color: Skin color, fun color, white

Wire: Underwire, no underwire

It's helpful to have multiple bras. Not only will they need to be washed, but it's also good to give a bra a rest and switch it up from day to day.

Some bras come in small, medium, and large sizes. However, many bras have a special sizing system that uses a number and a letter. The number is the band size, which is the size of your body (in inches) just below your breasts; the letter is the cup size (which we will explain how to figure out on page 56). An example of a bra size might be 30B.

You can buy bras at most stores that sell clothes, or you can go to a bra-only store and get measured by a professional. But it's okay if you're not comfortable doing that. You can measure yourself at home. Here's how.

Step 1: Measure your band size

* With your arms down by your sides, wearing an unpadded bra if needed to support your breasts, use a soft tape measure to measure your body all the way around snugly underneath your breasts. Write down this number in inches. This is your band size.

* Band sizes usually come in even numbers, so if the measurement is an odd number, your band size may either be one number up or one number down from your measurement. You may need to try both sizes to see which one fits best.

Step 2: Measure your bust size

* Without a bra, wrap the tape measuring loosely around your entire chest at the level of your nipples.

★ Round the measurement to the nearest whole number. This is your bust size.

Step 3: Calculate your cup size

★ Bust size – band size = cup size

★ Find the letter of your cup size in this chart, below the number.

Bust size minus band size (the difference in inches)	0	1	2	3	4
Cup size	AA	A	B	C	D

How do I know if my bra fits?

* It takes some getting used to, but it should be comfortable.

* It should not be poking or hurting anywhere.

* Adjusting the straps can help with the fit and prevent the straps from falling off your shoulders.

* The band around your ribs should stay in place.

* The cup should cover up most of your breast.

* If your bra has a hook in the back, you want your bra to initially fit on the outermost hook, because it will stretch out over time and you will want to be able to tighten it.

* You should be able to put one or two fingers under the band, but not your whole hand.

You don't have to wear a bra, but sometimes a good bra can make a difference in how you feel about your breasts as they are changing. Some people choose not to wear a bra, and that is okay, too. You get to make the decision that is right for you.

PUBIC HAIR

Pubic hair typically develops after breast budding begins. However, in 15 percent of girls, pubic hair will be the first sign of puberty. Pubic hair is hair that grows on your labia or pubic mound, which is the triangular part of your body between your legs. It grows in the area between your legs that your underwear covers.

Pubic hair is quite different than the hair on your head. It's thicker, coarser, curlier, and often darker. You will start to get just a few strands, and slowly grow more and more hair until it grows out toward your underwear creases. Pubic hair even grows a little onto the tops of your thighs.

What is the purpose of this hair? Pubic hair helps keep your vulva clean. It acts like a broom to help keep bacteria away from this sensitive area. The hair also helps keep vaginal discharge away from the skin, allowing your skin to stay dry.

We see patients in our office who want to remove their pubic hair. We understand it can be hard to get used to, and sometimes it seems like it would be easier if it weren't there. However, because pubic hair is different than the other hair on your body, when it grows back after shaving, it can become itchy or irritating. In addition, these types of coarse hairs can grow in incorrectly under the skin, causing ingrown hairs and infections.

There are ways to groom or trim your pubic hair if it's growing outside of your bathing suit bottoms. A safe and easy way to remove the edges of your pubic hair is with an electric razor. You can also carefully use small scissors and a mirror to trim it. It's important to steer clear of hair removal creams, because they are full of chemicals and can cause significant skin irritation.

Just as people have different styles of dressing, everyone feels differently about grooming their pubic hair. The important thing to know is that you get to decide, because you are the boss of your body.

YOUR VULVA

When you look in the mirror and see the upside-down triangular area between your legs, most people refer to this as the vagina. Technically, this is not correct. Your outside private parts are important and have their own name: **vulva.**

It is important to use the correct terms for all the parts of your body so we all know what we are talking about. You wouldn't call your nose your ear just because they are close together, right? When you use the correct anatomical terms for your body, you not only sound smart, but you also do not need to feel ashamed or embarrassed. All of us ladies have the same amazing parts.

Just like breasts, everyone's vulva will look a little bit different, and that is okay.

There are personal parts on the outside and on the inside of our bodies. Starting at the outside, the part you see when you are looking in the mirror is called the labia majora. Labia is Latin for "mouth." This part is made up of skin and is where your pubic hair grows. Inside, there are smaller labia, called the labia minora. These may be tucked inside the labia majora and harder to see, or they may be visible from the outside. Both variants are normal and healthy.

At the very top where the labia majora meet in the middle is your clitoris. The clitoris is the most sensitive area of your genitals; there are hundreds of nerve endings here. The area that projects upward is called the clitoral hood, but most of the clitoris is actually under the labia.

Under the clitoris is a small hole called the urethra. The urethra is the hole you pee out of. At the bottom, you have your anus, which is the hole you poop out of. The hole in between them leads to a tunnel that goes inside of your body, and this tunnel is your vagina.

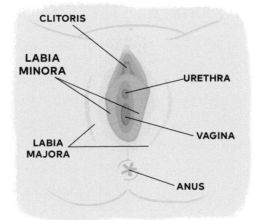

The vagina is a tunnel that connects to the uterus. Also called the womb, the uterus is a home for a fetus (an unborn baby). There are two ovaries on either side of the uterus that hold and release the eggs needed for reproduction (see chapter 7). Fallopian tubes carry the egg from the ovary to the uterus.

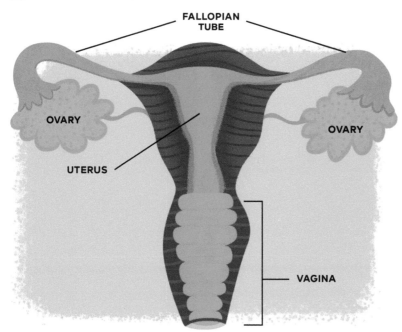

Care Down There

Just as you care for other parts of your body, your vulva needs your attention. The only thing your vulva needs from you is to make sure the skin in and around the folds of your legs is clean. You have special kinds of sweat glands here that cause body odor, so be sure to use soap and water in the creases and wash well. Your vagina takes care of cleaning itself; you don't need to clean inside the tunnel. There are thousands of healthy bacteria that live in your vagina, keeping it in happy harmony. Washing inside (also known as douching) disturbs these bacteria and can cause infections and irritation.

Giving your vulva area time to air out and breathe is very important. Some girls wear tight clothing that can be constricting. If this is something you do often, think about coming home, taking off your underwear, and grabbing a loose, comfy pair of pants to allow your vulva time to breathe. We recommend you sleep without underwear to keep your vagina healthy.

Vaginal Secretions

Many parts of your body have secretions. Can you think of some?

* Eyes ➜ tears

* Mouth ➜ saliva

* Nose ➜ mucus (snot)

Your vagina also secretes its own unique fluid. This is called **vaginal discharge**. This discharge looks and feels like the white part of a raw egg; it's often clear or milky white, and thick and gooey.

Most girls will start noticing some vaginal discharge as their body is developing. This discharge comes from your uterus and is its way of preparing for its next assignment. You typically won't see the discharge coming out of your vagina. You will likely see discharge in your underwear or notice some on the toilet paper when you are wiping.

The amount of discharge each girl has is unique to her body. Some girls have a lot of vaginal discharge—enough that they need to wear a small pad in their underwear to stay dry or change their underwear throughout the day. Other girls will barely have any at all. Either way, it's important to learn what is normal for you.

Your vaginal discharge may vary in amount and consistency, but it should not itch or have a significant color or odor. If this happens, talk to your parent about it. If you still have questions, you can always ask your doctor—that is what we are here for!

MENSTRUATION: THE BIG CHANGE

Without a doubt, the biggest change during puberty is the onset of menstruation—when you get your period. Your period is the time of each month that you bleed from your uterus through your vagina. It's an exciting time, as your body proves that it's working properly. There are many different terms people use to describe menstruation. You may hear people refer to it as "that time of the month" or "code red" or "a visit from Aunt Flo." No matter what you call it, it's a normal milestone in a girl's life that marks a big transition for your body.

Everyone gets their first period when it's right for their body. If you are an early bird, you may wish that you didn't get your period until later, and if you are a late bloomer, you may feel left out if all your friends have it before you. Either way, your body is making the decision about when this will happen. So you can prepare for it, but you don't get to decide when it will happen.

WHAT TO EXPECT

Everyone wants to know *exactly* when this big transition will happen, because it's easier if you are prepared. Unfortunately, there is no magic formula to tell you the exact date and time you will get your first period. You can use various clues to know where you are in puberty, so you will know if you are close to getting your period.

* **Body changes**. You will have breasts and pubic hair *before* you get your period. In fact, a period usually comes about two to two and half years *after* you get your first breast bud. The breast bud is the firm, peanut-like lump under your nipple.

* **Height**. Most girls have a large growth spurt just before their first period. Height change is something that's difficult to notice on yourself, but you may ask your doctor to look at your growth chart with you to see if you grew more than average this past year.

* **Vaginal discharge.** Most girls will have had some vaginal discharge before their first period.

* **Age.** The average age a girl in the United States gets her first period is 12½ years old. The typical range for a girl to get her first period is between ages 10 and 15.

* **Family history.** Ask the other women in your family when they started their periods. If it's possible, ask if your family members were early birds, late bloomers, or in-betweeners. Girls often follow in their female family's footsteps.

Why Do Women Have Periods?

The whole purpose of puberty is to get your body ready to reproduce, or to be able to make new people. Your period is the way your body prepares to get this job done. The menstrual cycle is a cycle that happens again and again to give your body lots of chances to eventually get pregnant.

Your body prepares for pregnancy every month. Your brain releases hormones to tell the ovaries to release an egg (a process called ovulation). This egg travels through the fallopian tubes to the uterus. While the egg is on its journey, the uterus starts making a safe, nurturing place for the egg to land. It's creating a lining on the inside of the uterus made out of blood. Under the right circumstances (see chapter 7), the egg can get fertilized by a sperm and start to develop into a baby.

Since most of the time we are not going to grow a baby, the uterus doesn't need the lining it built. So once a month the uterus sheds or gets rid of the lining. This is when the blood leaves the uterus and travels out a tunnel (your vagina) to exit your body. This is called getting your period.

The cycle, once it becomes regular, happens about every 21 to 45 days in a predictable pattern. However, this predictable pattern takes some time to develop. Initially, you may get your first period and then not get your next one for two or three months—or even longer. Your body is gearing up for a big job, and it takes some practice to get it right. It can take your hormones a couple of years to get organized and for your period to become regular and happen every month.

Anticipating getting your first period can be exciting if you know what to expect. Most girls picture a situation where they are standing in school and many people are looking at them, and all of a sudden they are standing in a pool of blood. We are happy to say this IS NOT the way it works! Instead, you may notice blood on the toilet paper when you are wiping or a stain of red or brown in the middle of your underwear.

Period FAQs

We know there are many, many questions about periods, so let's discuss the most common ones here.

How long will my period last?

On average, your period will last about five days each month. It's helpful to keep track of your period on a calendar or an app so you can see if it's becoming regular. This way you will know when to expect it. At the back of the book are some suggestions for useful technology tools to help with this.

Will it hurt?

Bleeding with your period doesn't hurt like bleeding from cutting your finger. Since your uterus is a muscle, you can sometimes get cramping from the uterus squeezing. Uterine cramps feel like getting a cramp in your leg—only it's in your lower abdomen.

How much will I bleed during a period?

The amount a woman bleeds with her period varies from person to person. It can be just a few tablespoons over a week, to about two ounces during each period. The amount you bleed is referred to as your flow. Days when there is just a little bleeding are called light flow, and days with more bleeding are called heavy flow. Most periods start off heavy in the first few days and then become lighter. It's a good idea to fill up a measuring cup with water with these amounts so you can get an idea of how little blood there actually is!

What happens if I get my period at school?

This can happen and you will be fine. We are going to help you be prepared. If you have started puberty, you should have some backup supplies so you are ready. We recommend keeping a bag with supplies in your locker or in your backpack in case you get your period at school.

Here are our recommendations for a period pack:

★ Clean pair of underwear

★ Maxipad or pantyliner

★ Towelette or wipe

★ Plastic bag for soiled underwear

If you don't have your period pack, you can always ask a female teacher for help or supplies. Remember, *all* women have had their period before, so they understand and are willing to help.

What if I get blood on my underwear or bed sheets?

Period stains on your underwear are common and should be expected. You don't need to throw something out every time you get a period stain, but you should take care of it right away so the blood will not cause a permanent stain. You can rinse your underwear with some laundry detergent and cold water in the sink. Hydrogen peroxide also helps get blood out of clothing.

How much time is normal between periods?

The average menstrual cycle is 28 days, but a normal cycle can range from 21 days to 45 days between the start of one period and the start of your next period. That means it may not begin on the exact same date of each month.

What if I don't ever get my period or I skip a couple of periods in a row?

These are excellent questions but likely relate to issues that are specific to you. We recommend you discuss this with your doctor. Sometimes you don't get your period because you may not have enough body fat to support the process of ovulation and menstruation. Healthy nutrition helps support a healthy menstrual cycle.

COOL AND CONFIDENT

It's okay to fail. No one is perfect, and even the most successful people you know have had many failures. You may fail a test, or you may not make a team that you tried out for, and that's okay. Perseverance means that you keep trying despite the outcome. It's a hard life lesson to learn, but it's important to focus more on your effort than on the outcome. Mastering a skill builds confidence, but it takes time to be good at something. This applies to academics, music, sports, cooking, and anything in life! Learn how to fail and keep trying, while still loving yourself.

PADS, TAMPONS, AND PERIOD CARE

You are going to have your period for many days of your life while you are out there becoming who you want to be, and your period should not be something that holds you back. Thankfully, there are a variety of products to choose from so you don't have to skip any activities when you have your period. Many stores have an entire aisle of what they call feminine hygiene products or menstrual care products—products made just for period care. The goal is for you to be comfortable, clean, and worry-free during menstruation.

Pads and tampons are the two most common products girls use to take care of their menstrual bleeding. Pads are absorbent liners worn in your underwear to soak up the blood coming out of your vagina. Tampons are cotton plugs that you insert into your vagina to catch the blood before it leaves your body. You don't have to choose just one type of product. You may use different products depending on the situation. Pads are easy and are the most common product to start with when you first get your period. Tampons require a bit more learning, and it takes time to get comfortable using them.

What you use depends on your activity and your personal preference. It's like deciding what kind of backpack or purse you like to carry. Not everyone likes the same things. For example, wearing a leotard or bathing suit may require you to figure out how to use a tampon quicker than your best friend, who doesn't do gymnastics or swim. A vacation for a week at the beach may change your mind about trying tampons.

Another feminine hygiene product is a menstrual cup. This is a reusable device that you insert into your vagina to collect the blood, rather than absorb it. You then remove the cup from your vagina periodically throughout the day, empty it, rinse and clean it, and then reinsert it back into the vagina. It's much more environmentally friendly than pads or tampons, but it's often not used by beginners. Inserting a menstrual cup requires you to be very comfortable with your body.

Reusable, washable underwear that absorbs the blood from your period is another great option. These can replace pads or tampons or menstrual cups, or even be worn along with them for extra protection. There are many brands and styles to choose from, such as Thinx, Knix, and Ruby Love.

How to Use Pads

Pads come in different thicknesses, absorbencies, and shapes. Thanks to technology, even some thin pads can absorb a lot of blood, so it's no longer true that a thick pad is required for good absorption. Some really absorbent pads are thin or even ultrathin. On the bottom of most pads is a sticky side to secure the pad to your underwear.

PERIOD PAD POSSIBILITIES

Thickness: Ultrathin, Thin, Regular, Thick
Absorbency: Light, Moderate, Heavy, Overnight
Shape: With wings, Thong, Long

On the outside of the package, there will be an absorbency rating. This will let you know if the pad is for light flow, moderate (average) flow, or heavy flow. If your flow is heavy, you will want a pad that is more absorbent, such as a heavy or overnight pad. If you have a lighter period with a minimal amount of blood, you can use a lighter pad, sometimes called a pantyliner.

Since bodies have different shapes and everyone has different preferences, there are lots of different pad shapes. Some pads have wings—sides that wrap around the crotch of your panties—for better stain protection.

You can use any of these types of pads on any day or at any time that is right for you! You will likely find you need different types of pads for different days of your periods, and perhaps for different times of day as well (day versus night).

Most women use disposable menstrual pads (also known as maxipads), but you can also use reusable cloth pads that can be washed. Reusable pads are much kinder to our environment.

Step-by-Step Instructions for How to Use a Pad

1. Find a bathroom. Wash your hands.

2. Get in position. It's easiest to have your underwear around your knees and within arms' reach.

3. Remove the wrapper from the pad and use the wrapper to help wrap up the old pad you are throwing out in the garbage. (DO NOT ever try to flush a pad down a toilet.)

4. If the sticky part of the pad already isn't exposed, remove the paper on the back to uncover the sticky strip.

5. Stick the pad in your underwear with thoughtful aim. You want it pretty much in the center so it's directly under your vagina when you put your underwear back on. You can always rearrange it if you don't get it perfect on the first try.

6. If the pad has wings, wrap them around the sides of your underwear.

7. Wash your hands.

8. Change your pad at least every four hours, or more often if needed, so you can stay clean and fresh.

How to Use Tampons

Once a tampon is inserted in the vagina, it stays in place and soaks up the blood until you take it out. You pull it out by a string that hangs outside your body. It does not hurt to put in, wear, or remove a tampon. There is no seal on your vagina, so a tampon will not break anything.

Tampons also come in a variety of sizes and absorbencies. There are light tampons for light flow days, regular for moderate flow days, and super absorbent tampons for heavy flow days. There are also scented tampons, but we do not recommend them because they can irritate your vagina.

It's important to be responsible and change your tampon every four to six hours. If you leave a tampon inside your vagina for too long, bacteria can grow and cause an infection. This illness is called toxic shock syndrome (TSS) and can be serious. For this reason, we do not recommend sleeping overnight with a tampon.

There is no particular age you have to be to wear a tampon. However, if you want to try to use a tampon, you should:

★ Be comfortable with the word vagina, and know where yours is.

★ Be comfortable touching your vagina, because that's how you have to put it in.

* Be responsible and remember to change your tampon every four to six hours.

You also have to have enough flow to use a tampon. If your menstrual flow is very light, then using a tampon can be uncomfortable because there is not enough lubrication for the tampon to go in and out easily.

Step-by-Step Instructions for How to Use a Tampon with an Applicator

1. Find a bathroom. Wash your hands. It can be helpful to use a handheld mirror the first time to help you.

2. Get in position. The best options are to either to sit on the toilet with your legs spread apart or put one leg up on the toilet.

3. Remove the tampon wrapper. Keep the tampon inside the applicator.

4. Relax. Learning how to relax your muscles in your pelvis and vagina makes this easier (see the box on page 82).

5. Hold the tampon in your dominant hand between your thumb and middle finger on the grip section of the applicator, with your pointer finger on the end of the plunger.

6. Insert the applicator into your vagina until your thumb and middle finger touch your body. Aim toward your lower back, not toward your brain.

7. Gently use your pointer finger to push the plunger in, which pushes the tampon deeper into your vagina. Push the plunger until the ends of both tubes are even.

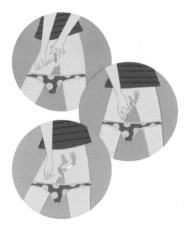

8. Pull the applicator out of your vagina. The tampon should stay in your vagina with the string hanging outside. It should not hurt or be uncomfortable.

9. Throw out the applicator in the garbage. If you removed a tampon, make sure to wrap it in toilet paper and throw it into the garbage too. Don't flush used tampons down the toilet.

10. Wash your hands.

11. Change your tampon at least every four to six hours, or more often if needed.

RELAX!

The walls of your vagina are made of muscles called the pelvic floor muscles. Just like any other muscle in your body, the muscles of your vagina can contract (tighten) or relax. One way to learn how your pelvic floor muscles work is to start and stop your urine stream while you are peeing. You can feel your muscles tighten to stop peeing, and relax to continue peeing. Now try doing that while sitting here and reading this book. You can just tighten and relax those muscles anytime—even in the middle of math class. These are called Kegel exercises. These exercises will help you learn how to relax when you put in a tampon. It's important! When you are tense, your vaginal muscles will clench together and make the vaginal opening and tunnel tight.

Step-by-Step Instructions for How to Use a Tampon Without an Applicator

1. Find a bathroom. Wash your hands. It can be helpful to use a handheld mirror the first time to help you.

2. Get in position. The best options are to either to sit on the toilet with your legs spread apart or put one leg up on the toilet.

3. Remove the tampon wrapper. Make sure the string is securely attached to the tampon and is hanging downward.

4. Relax. Learning how to relax your muscles in your pelvis and vagina helps a lot (see the box on page 82).

5. Hold the tampon in your dominant hand. With your other hand, spread your labia (the fleshy lips that protect your vagina).

6. Gently push the tampon into your vagina, aiming toward your lower back (not your brain). You will need to push it deeper using your index finger.

7. The tampon should stay in your vagina with the string hanging outside. It should not hurt or be uncomfortable.

8. If you removed a tampon, make sure to wrap it in toilet paper and throw it into the garbage. Don't flush used tampons down the toilet.

9. Wash your hands.

10. Change your tampon at least every four to six hours, or more often if needed.

Shopping for Supplies

Going to the drugstore when you first get your period can be exciting but also overwhelming. How is a smart girl supposed to know what to buy to take care of her period when there are so many choices in the feminine care aisle at the store? The best thing to do is buy a few different types of products (or raid your mom's bathroom closet, with permission) so you can touch, feel, and get to know what each option is like.

Feminine care is a constantly expanding aisle at the store, with choices for just about every situation. There are even some products now that are made exclusively for teens, sized appropriately for your body (and of course they are packaged cuter too!).

But first things first: Don't be embarrassed to buy your supplies. Just as every kid needs school supplies for school, every girl eventually needs period supplies for her period. It's best to keep a few different choices at home to meet your needs, which may change depending on the day and flow of your period. Over time you will find your favorite brands and products, and, hopefully, become comfortable enough with your body to try new products. For your first time using tampons or pads, feel free to open and inspect them to get to know how they work before you try to use them.

PMS AND OTHER PERIOD PALS

Having periods means you are getting older and more mature, and your body is changing just as it was meant to do. Taking care of your period can take some getting used to, but in time you will be good at knowing what you need. Period care is not just about dealing with the flow of blood, though. There are other issues that can go along with your period that you should know about.

Cramps

Dysmenorrhea, also known as period cramps, is something almost every girl experiences at one time or another. Remember, the uterus is a giant muscle that has to contract to squeeze the blood out. Your uterus tightening and relaxing can feel uncomfortable sometimes. Period cramps can feel like a stomachache or can feel like back pain.

The good news is that period cramps respond very well to heating pads and over-the-counter medicines like ibuprofen. Talk to your parents about taking something for period cramps if you are not feeling well. If that doesn't do the trick, it's time to talk to your doctor. We have lots of options for you!

PMS

Premenstrual syndrome (PMS) is a term for a variety of physical and emotional symptoms you may experience about one to two weeks before you get your period each month. While scientists haven't discovered the exact reason why women get PMS, it's generally thought to be because of the changing hormone levels during your menstrual cycle. About three-quarters of women report they get some type of PMS symptoms with their menstrual cycle.

There are a lot of different things women report as PMS symptoms. Physically you may experience bloating (feeling like your stomach is too full), lower abdominal (pelvic) pain, back pain, headaches, breast swelling and tenderness, food cravings, fatigue, and acne. Mentally you may feel moodier and emotionally sensitive (also known as mood swings).

Yes, that's a long list of symptoms, but you won't experience all of these at the same time. Some girls actually will barely have any symptoms! These symptoms can change from month to month or be consistent signs that your period is coming soon.

Ways to minimize PMS symptoms:

* Good nutrition

* Exercise

* Hydration (with water, avoid caffeine)

* Managing stress

* Eating healthy foods

* Ibuprofen and a heating pad for cramping

* Getting enough sleep

You should not have to miss school or activities regularly due to your period. Can you imagine if famous athletes had to miss their competitions because of period symptoms, or successful businesswomen didn't show up to run their companies because of PMS? You got this! It just takes knowledge and a willingness to take care of yourself and to ask for help when you need it. If you feel like you're missing more activities than you should, check in with your parent or a doctor.

YOUR AMAZING BRAIN

• •

We have discussed a lot of important things happening to your body during puberty, but there is just as much happening in your brain. This time in your life brings physical change *and* cognitive (thinking) and emotional change. Although your brain has grown to almost its full size by the time you start kindergarten, during adolescence your brain is going through a lot of remodeling and rearranging. These changes affect both the structure and function of your brain. It will take many years to complete these important renovations, but in the end, you will be stronger, smarter, and more sophisticated.

BRAIN ANATOMY

Warning: Important science lesson ahead . . . but keep reading!

Let's look at your basic brain anatomy. There are, of course, many different parts of your brain, and each part has a very specific job. We'd like to introduce you to just a few parts that play key roles in your teen brain.

Amygdala/limbic system (deep inside your brain)

* Your emotional center

* The most dominant part of a teen brain

Prefrontal cortex (at the front of your brain)

* Judgment and decisions

* Organization center

* Your source of logic and reason

The brain develops from the back to the front and from the inside out. Your limbic system, which is in charge of your emotions, lies deep in the center of your brain. Since it develops first, it allows you to feel the wide range of emotions that comes with growing up. Your prefrontal cortex on the other hand, is in the front and outside portion of the brain, so it develops *last*. This leaves the emotional center in control during your teen years.

Teens tend to make decisions based on emotions, rather than with their prefrontal cortex, which makes decisions based on thoughtful reasoning of pros and cons. Emotional decisions are not always the best decisions. Unfortunately, your prefrontal cortex isn't fully online until around age 25, so there is a good reason your parents are constantly telling you to be careful and think before you act.

While your brain is under construction, it follows the basic "use it or lose it" policy. Therefore, it's important as a teen to use different parts of your brain. Playing an instrument, reading books, and learning to play a sport will form strong, useful  connections in different parts of your brain. Take the time to learn new skills and exercise your brain, because the parts that go unused are trimmed away. For example, if you learned Spanish as a young child and were fluent in the language, and then you stopped speaking Spanish during your teen years, you would actually lose this knowledge over time. It would be pruned out of your brain. So if you have a skill you want to keep, you have to keep practicing and using it.

TECHNOLOGY AND THE TEENAGE BRAIN

Technology can have profound effects on your brain. It can alter the connections and chemicals in your brain, and therefore the way you communicate and function. Most girls want access to more technology as they get older. It's a good way to gain independence while still staying connected to your family and friends. There are many amazing things that can come from having the world at your fingertips; but with this power comes responsibility. It's your job to use your tech judiciously and develop good habits early. Every family handles technology-use differently, but here are some guidelines that are good for your brain and will also help keep you safe.

Using Technology

You may not have access to any device, you may have a shared family device, or you may have your own device. Your family may have many technology rules or no rules at all. Either way, as you are getting older, it's your job to use technology to enhance your life, not to take away from it. Don't let technology cause fights with friends, lower your self-esteem, or interfere with your health.

Common Issues with Teens and Technology

Problem	Explanation	Solution
Interference with sleep	The light on your cell phone is known to cause issues with sleep. It actually prevents your brain from releasing its own sleep hormone (melatonin).	Stop using your cell phone one to two hours before bed. Plug in your cell phone in a different room than where you sleep. P.S. You can get a new alarm clock.
Interference with emotional processing	You are meant to feel a wide range of emotions. Some of these emotions can make you feel uncomfortable. To get better at dealing with them, you have to face them and not hide behind your technology.	When you are anxious or bored, don't always reach for your device. Think about going on a walk or connecting with a family member or friend.
FOMO (Fear of Missing Out)	This is a big one. Knowing what your friends are doing while they are actually doing it can be . . . well . . . hard. There are going to be times when you feel as if you have been left out.	Remember, technology is supposed to help you connect with others, not constantly remind you of what you are missing. If technology is making you feel bad while you are on it, limit its use. Or better yet, hang out *in real life* with people who make you forget about using your tech.

Using Social Media

We know it's important for you to be connected with your friends. Your parents may not have had cell phones when they were young, but they took their home phone with a long cord and stretched it as far as it could reach into their bedroom so they could spend hours chatting with their friends. Today, communication with friends is easier than ever. You can use text messaging and social media—or (gasp!) pick up the phone and call a friend anytime you want to. You can even use phone apps to see where your friends are at all times.

Using this technology to stay connected affects your teen brain differently than an adult brain. The people who create apps know this, and you are their target audience! It's very easy to become addicted to the feeling you get when someone likes something you posted. This positive feedback is rewarding, and it's not a feeling that happens as often when talking to a friend in real life. Each buzz of your device gives a little thrill to your brain, keeping you engaged. But just like anything else, too much of a good thing can be bad. If you find that you are constantly checking your phone for validation from your friends, you should rethink your technology use.

WARNING SIGNS OF TECHNOLOGY ADDICTION

★ Does being separated from your cell phone cause you anxiety?

★ Are you neglecting other areas of your life to be on your cell phone?

★ Are you spending more than two hours per day on social media?

★ Do you have more friendships online than offline?

★ Is your cell phone isolating you from others in real life?

★ Does your cell phone interfere with your sleep or your self-care?

★ Do you prefer your cell phone over your friends or activities?

If you answered yes to one or more of these questions, it's time to reevaluate your use of technology. You need to limit how much you use your device; the settings on your cell phone can help you with this.

EMOTIONAL UPS AND DOWNS

Mood swings are when you have an abrupt change in your mood, sometimes for no apparent reason. At times your emotions can feel extra intense and out of control. You may get teary for no reason, feel sensitive to even the smallest of criticisms, or be smiling from ear to ear just because a friend invited you over. Remember that feelings don't last forever; they will come and go quickly. Adolescence—the time between you not being a kid anymore and the time before you are an adult—is full of a lot of emotional ups and downs.

Your brain has many jobs, one of which is to release hormones. Hormones are powerful chemical messengers that not only physically change parts of your body but are also responsible for amplifying your moods. Frequent fluctuations in hormone levels (which happens during puberty) cause emotions to be louder and more dramatic than they otherwise would be.

Your mood is also influenced by people and things in your environment. For example, you can be in a bad mood because you have a disagreement with your parent in the car on your way to school. Your friends notice you are in a bad mood at school because you are less talkative than usual. But what if your day started differently? What if on the car ride to school your favorite song was playing on the radio, the sun was shining, and there was no disagreement? Your morning at school would be much different. Factors in your environment definitely affect your mood.

As a teen, emotional outbursts are common, and you may feel as if your emotions get the best of you. This is normal and expected. The emotional outbursts are like fireworks exploding in the emotional center of the brain. You have to wait for the explosion to run its course, knowing that the calm will follow. As you get older, you will become more familiar with the pattern of these outbursts and will develop ways of controlling and working through them. This enables you to become better at managing your feelings and making decisions based on logic rather than emotions.

How to Identify and Manage Your Emotions

What can you do to help manage this emotional rollercoaster? **It starts with identifying your emotions.** If you can name your different feelings, you have a better chance of learning how to deal with each one.

For example, you can probably think of a time (or many times!) you felt frustrated. Let's say you are frustrated because your mom was running late and dropped you off at your friend's party an hour late. What are your choices to deal with your anger and frustration?

1. **Yell and scream** (hint: not the right choice): This is the default because it's what you would want to do if your actions didn't affect anyone else. This approach

puts the person on the receiving end of your tantrum on the defensive. Your mom will get mad and will not appreciate your disrespectful tone, and the next time you want a ride, you might be out of luck.

2. **Physical violence** (hint: not the right choice): You could use your hands to actually hit the person you are mad at. We all know this would not end well. Enough said.

3. **Breathe and then speak** (hint: correct answer!): Take a deep breath. Exhale slowly. You can even count out loud if it will help you stay calm. Identify your emotion (frustration), gather your thoughts, and then speak calmly. You could try saying, "Mom, I'm so frustrated that I had to be late to this party because of your schedule. Thanks for getting me here, but next time can we plan ahead of time so I am not late?" If this seems like it would be difficult to do, *it is*! Not allowing your emotions to get the best of you is something that takes a lifetime to master. It's a skill, and like any other skill, it takes practice. You will not get it right every time, but you can get better at it with time and practice.

Growing up is a time to learn not only how to identify your feelings but also how to separate your feelings from your actions. Emotional control is one of the GOALS of adolescence.

What can you do to cope with your frequently changing emotions?

★ Take time to breathe (practice slow, deep breaths).

★ Make lists to help organize your thoughts and life.

★ Choose to do a self-care activity (for example, listen to music, exercise, take a bath, read a book . . . what's YOUR outlet?).

★ When you feel overwhelmed, take it one step at a time, one day at a time.

★ Find a trusted adult to talk to.

★ Write in a journal.

★ Get a good night's sleep.

There is one thing for certain that you should NOT do while feeling emotional: Do not turn to technology to deal (or not deal) with your hurt feelings. Immediately texting something or posting something to social media does not give you time to think. You may share something that you regret, because technology instantly shares information that cannot be taken back. Give yourself time to process what happened and how you feel about it. Try instead to write your feelings down on paper, because an hour later, or a day later, you may feel that you don't want to share those feelings at all.

COOL AND CONFIDENT

There are ways to train your brain to make yourself stronger emotionally. Just like learning any skill, it takes time and practice. Since you were not born with big biceps muscles in your arms, if you want nice arm muscles you have to exercise and train hard. This is the same thing you need to do with your brain. Being strong mentally means you have to flex your brain muscles.

WHEN FEELINGS GET OUT OF CONTROL

The words stress, anxiety, and depression are used a lot in today's world. It's important to learn about these concepts so you can understand more about yourself and your feelings.

STRESS is pressure you feel from external demanding circumstances. This can relate to school, friends, or extracurricular activities.

ANXIETY is your emotional reaction to stress. It might be nervousness or persistent worry.

We can use these terms interchangeably because they so often hang out together. Everyone has some stress and it's often a part of everyday life. Stress can cause you to feel anxiety—a feeling of nervousness and fear that makes you feel uncomfortable. Depending on the severity, stress and anxiety can be healthy or unhealthy.

Healthy stress is a motivator that helps you get things done and accomplish your goals. It helps you challenge yourself, push past your limits, and grow. In fact, stress is actually hardwired in your brain to keep you safe. If you are on a peaceful hike in the woods, for instance, and you see a big bear, your stress system warns you of potential danger to help you stay safe.

Today, it's not often that you encounter a bear as a source of your stress, but you will probably have an argument with a friend or perform poorly on an exam. You need to step back and identify this emotion, feel it, act appropriately on it, and move on. For example, if you are anxious about an upcoming test and you are not prepared, your feelings are a message to you to do something about it (go study!). If your stress is about a conflict with a friend, you can use it as a signal to find ways to work through it.

Chronic stress is stress that continues without any break. People who live in dangerous environments where their well-being is threatened can feel chronic stress. Recently, however, there are more and more girls who feel chronic stress despite being in safe environments. These girls don't give themselves time to take breaks from their stress. They may be overscheduled with school and activities and have no downtime. Continuous stress without breaks is unhealthy because there is no time for your brain and body to recover.

If you feel stressed and you don't know why, or your anxiety interferes with your ability to function normally, you need to look for some help managing it. Unhealthy amounts of stress and anxiety can give you physical symptoms like stomachaches and sleep problems, and emotional symptoms like concentration problems and irritability. You want to be in control of your stress and anxiety, not let them control you.

We want to introduce you to a word that many girls may not know: rumination. Rumination is overthinking a situation. Your thoughts sometimes become a runaway train. Sometimes people refer to this as "being in your own head."

Girls often repetitively think about the same situation over and over again, which can cause anxiety. What can you do to avoid ruminating? Give yourself an assigned time to think about a situation, and then be done. Just being aware that you may tend to ruminate can be a helpful way to decrease this type of stressful behavior.

SADNESS AND DEPRESSION

It's perfectly normal to feel sad sometimes. You may feel sad because you weren't included in a night out with friends that you saw posted on social media, or because someone you love isn't feeling well. Take time to be sad about the situation, and use your best coping skills.

True clinical depression is a different story. It's not just being temporarily sad about a specific situation; it's when you are sad most of the time, unrelated to any particular situation. You no longer enjoy activities or spending time with people you used to enjoy. You may have trouble sleeping, a change in appetite, or new academic problems.

Depression can affect anyone, any age, and at any time. You don't need to suffer alone or be ashamed for feeling this way. If you feel this way, you need to talk to a trusted adult or a health professional who specializes in emotions. It may feel like no one cares, but those who love you do care about your mental health.

YOUR INNER VOICE

Your inner voice is the voice in your head that is always talking to you. Hopefully, this voice compliments your accomplishments. For example, your inner voice may say, "I just rocked my band concert. I had the best performance ever!"

But sometimes you may find that your inner voice is harsh or overly critical. It may say, "I have the same shirt as her, but why does she look cuter in it than me?" Remember, *you are your inner voice*, so you can control its narrative. If you wouldn't say something to a friend, then you shouldn't say it to yourself. We want you to turn up the volume on your nice inner voice, and change the channel when your mean inner voice tries to bring you down. You, just like all people, are a work in progress. Practice using positive self-talk. Your inner voice should be your own best friend.

Don't be a victim of negative self-talk. Remember, you are listening.

–BOB PROCTOR

ASKING FOR HELP

It's important to know that everyone struggles with moods at some point. You are not alone. When you are having a hard time emotionally, it's okay to ask for help.

How can you find someone to help you? Start by identifying the people in your life who provide you with support. Everyone needs a trusted adult who can offer emotional support. A trusted adult should be a good listener and someone who will believe what you are saying. Your trusted adults want you to be safe, healthy, and happy.

Your trusted adult should be someone you feel safe with. They should not make you feel scared or ask you to keep secrets. Take the time right now to identify the trusted adults in your life. Some possibilities include:

* Parents
* Relatives
* Teachers
* School counselors

* Coaches
* Mentors
* Doctors

Talking to a trusted adult or a good friend can help you make a game plan and feel less alone. Better yet, talk to someone who makes you laugh! Simply finding your smile can turn your day around.

Staying active and exercising can also help you manage stress and moods. Getting your body moving energizes you and releases some physical tension. Activities you enjoy, whether it's art, music, or sports, can help you feel better physically and mentally.

Practicing Mindfulness

Practicing mindfulness can be really helpful in dealing with stress and anxiety. Mindfulness is simply noticing what is happening right now and how you are feeling at this moment. It's taking the time to notice how your body feels

and what your mind sees and hears. It can help stop you from ruminating and prevent you from getting overwhelmed by giving yourself a space to think and relax.

There are many ways to practice mindfulness. Some people learn how to focus on their breathing; others choose yoga or meditation. Meditation is when you quiet your mind to help you relax. This is a skill that takes practice, and you can consider using some tools we list in the back of the book to help you get started.

HOW TO PRACTICE MINDFULNESS IN EVERYDAY LIFE

Designate a time and space for a technology-free zone. When you have fewer distractions, you can more easily focus on being mindful and aware of your feelings.

Pay full attention to the task at hand. Instead of having a conversation while doing your homework and listening to music, do one thing at a time and be mindful of that activity.

Pay attention to your senses. Name something at that moment that you can see, smell, hear, feel, or taste. (Taste your toothpaste when you brush your teeth, smell your shampoo in your shower, feel your feet in your shoes as you walk.)

Seek Out a Professional

There are some situations that cannot be fixed by talking to a friend, practicing mindfulness, or by getting a good night's sleep. There are millions of people all over the world who have mental health struggles. About half of you reading this book will need some extra support. There are a wide variety of mental health professionals to help guide you if you have concerns. Social workers, psychologists, psychiatrists, and your family doctor all have training to help you. Your trusted adult or school counselor can help you find the right professional for you. In the back of your book, we listed some websites to help you find the support you need.

Here are some warning signs that you might need professional help.

★ Nothing brings you joy or happiness.

★ You feel alone and like you have no friends.

★ You aren't motivated to do anything.

★ You feel anxious or sad all the time.

★ You feel unsafe in your environment.

★ You have thoughts about harming yourself or others.

Most people don't know what to expect when they need to visit a mental health professional. In simplest terms, they are talking doctors. You should not be afraid to talk to a mental health professional or feel as if there is something wrong with you. It just means you need a little extra help. If you broke your arm, you would see a doctor to help you fix it. Instead of getting an arm cast in the office, you spend time in the office talking about your feelings and ways to help manage them.

Therapists are different than talking to your BFF or parents because they are not biased, are not a part of your everyday life, and are obligated to keep your information completely confidential. Your parents and friends don't have the same training as a professional. Don't hesitate to reach out for help if you need it.

RELATIONSHIPS

Puberty is a time of social change as well as physical and emotional change. Just as your body physically goes through puberty at its own pace, girls also develop socially at different times. Through all of these changes, the number one rule is to stay true to yourself. Stay confident and continue to transform yourself into who YOU want to be.

In your lifetime, you will have a lot of different types of relationships. You will develop unique relationships with your parents, siblings, friends, teachers, coaches, and more. Each of these connections will have different meanings, but the goal is for each one to be a healthy and positive addition to your life. Relationships should help make you a better person. Take advantage of learning from each relationship to enhance future connections.

Healthy relationships should include:

* Respect

* Communication (be a good listener!)

* Honesty

* Mutual support

* Being able to be yourself

* Feeling good about yourself

* Equality

* Trust

You deserve this.

Relationships are complicated and not always perfect, but they should not be filled with constant hurt. There are times in any relationship that you may disagree or be upset. It may feel like a tug of war of give and take sometimes—but really, no one needs to win. It's important to give and receive different things out of each of your relationships and appreciate each one for what it brings to your life. If you feel threatened, intimidated, or are constantly being made to feel bad, then you have an unhealthy relationship. There are references in the back of the book to help you seek help if you're in a relationship that's not good for you.

FRIENDSHIPS AND CONFLICTS

Adolescence means you are becoming more independent, separating from your parents and trying to find your own people. You will likely find that you want to spend less time with your family and more time with your friends. It's very natural to want to try to fit into a group of people. Friends can be fabulous and fun, but they can also be tricky.

Quality trumps quantity in the friendship department. Having one or two really great friendships can be very fulfilling and may be all you need to feel connected. Having a lot of friends can be fun, but it may lead to superficial relationships and prevent you from developing deeper relationships that can enhance your life. It's also important to remember that good friends can be of the opposite gender. Boy-and-girl relationships don't always have to be about romance.

Most teens have friends in all of these categories. You may have one or two close friends to confide in, and then a web of friends on the periphery who can add both fun and, sometimes, drama to your life.

Even though friendships are wonderful, expect that there will be conflict. Remember, it's impossible for everyone to like you all the time. If you are striving for this, you will fall short every time. Conflict between friends is normal, and there are ways to work through it. You don't always have to win a fight or agree with a friend. You can agree to disagree and move on. Standing up for yourself means that you respect yourself and are setting healthy boundaries in relationships. But while you are doing that, try to show others the respect you would want. Ultimately, the only person you are in control of is yourself.

It's important to realize that friends can sometimes hurt each other, but there is always an option to apologize and forgive each other. Also remember that as people grow up, their interests change, and sometimes their groups of friends change. Just because you love to do everything with your best friend in fifth grade doesn't mean that will be the case in sixth grade. It's okay to outgrow a friendship and move in different directions.

The best friendships are the ones where you feel relaxed and like you can be yourself. Have you ever been in a group and felt nervous that you were going to say the wrong thing? Or do you fear people won't like you if you don't act "cool"? Those are not your friends. But your real friends are out there somewhere. When you find them, you will feel relaxed and comfortable with them—and with yourself. You won't feel as if you have to pretend, because these friends will accept you for who you are. If you don't find your true friends in your school class, maybe you'll find them in extracurricular activities, at your house of worship, or even at a different school.

Cliques

A group of people who hang out together is often referred to as a clique (pronounced "click"). While many people think a clique is a close-knit group of friends, this is not always the case. A clique can form from a common interest, like dance, or based on preferences, like the kind of clothes you wear.

Unfortunately, cliques tend to exclude other people and control who gets to be in the group and who gets left out. Your good friend may choose, or get chosen, to be a part of the clique. She may act differently toward you around her new friends, just to fit in, and then act like her normal self when you hang out just the two of you.

Remember, being true to yourself means not losing your identity as an individual if you are part of a clique. Having a group of friends you rely on is great, but a little kindness goes a long way when it's extended to someone outside your group. If a clique isn't your thing, being a friendly floater means you can enjoy the benefits of having different types of friends.

Peer Pressure

Peer pressure is when you feel like you have to behave a certain way because your peers (friends) expect it. Peer groups can shape your likes and dislikes and can influence you in positive or negative ways.

An example of positive peer pressure is when your friends encourage you to try out for the school sports team; maybe you would never have gone to try-outs if your friends didn't put some positive pressure on you. Another example is a group of girls who push each other to do their best in school.

Negative peer pressure is when your peer group forces you to do something you don't want to do. This is when people in a group influence one another to take risks that may even land them in an unsafe situation.

Often this type of pressure comes from people who don't respect you. An example of negative peer pressure is being asked to help a friend cheat on a test.

Sometimes peer pressure can be hard to recognize in the moment. Try to remember to listen to your *intuition*, or your gut. It's that feeling in your stomach that something is just not right, and it's a sign that you are doing something that goes against your core values. Your intuition is your built-in safety tool and moral compass.

Plan ahead for what you will do if you're in a negative peer pressure situation and don't want to follow the crowd. First, get comfortable saying "no." You don't owe anyone an explanation for why you won't do something you aren't comfortable with, but you can have some backup phrases handy. For example, you can blame your parents and say something like, "Nope! I can't do that. If my mom found out, I would never be allowed to hang with you guys again."

If you get caught in a sticky situation, it may help to have a code word you can use with your parents. For example, you could ask your parents, "How's the dog feeling?" and they will know it's time to come get you. Remember, you probably aren't the only one feeling uneasy. Your response may help save a friend too.

Managing peer influence means finding a balance between being yourself and fitting in. Your peer group matters, so choose your friends wisely.

FINDING YOUR IDENTITY

As you move into adolescence, you are forming your own identity. Everything from your hobbies to your hair color contribute to your identity. Your relationships and those you choose to surround yourself with will strongly influence your personal character. Your thoughts and actions are trying to answer the question: *Who am I?*

You will spend many years trying on different identities to find which one fits just right. It's a lot like picking out a new outfit: You can spend time trying on a bunch of different things, but when you find the right one, you light up. The same thing will happen with your identity. When you are uniquely you, you will shine. The quest to find your identity is a long journey that will require you to stand firm with your truths and be honest with yourself.

BElieve in **YOU**rself.

CHANGING FAMILY ROLES

Not all families are the same. You may have a different role in your family than your friend does in theirs. We hope your family can be a safe space for questions, emotional growth, support, and unconditional love. Even when it is, though, relationships with your family can become trickier to navigate at your age, and your role in your family may change over time. Your parents may expect more from you now that you are older.

As you become more independent, your opinions will change. Your new thoughts may not always align with your parents' opinions. This may include your opinions on politics or your curfew. You may feel you are ready for more responsibilities because you are older. Your parents may disagree or might not be ready to let you grow up so fast. This period of rapid change is hard for everyone and takes time to adjust to. Our best advice is to talk through the conflicts. Everyone has a right to their opinion and to be heard. Your parents' job is to make rules to help keep you safe, and you don't always have to like them.

When you were young, you may have thought your parents knew the answer to everything. As a teen, you may now think they know nothing. The truth probably lies somewhere in the middle. By now you have figured out that many questions don't have right or wrong answers, but shades of gray.

If you have siblings, your bond with them will change too. Some days you will feel like putting a KEEP OUT sign on your door and want nothing to do with your siblings, and other days you will be best friends and maybe even talk about how to handle a family conflict together. If you are an older sibling, you constantly have little eyes looking up to you, so remember to be a good role model.

Families can be complicated. The people you grow up with, especially the people you live with, help make you the person you become. They will be there for you for the long haul. It's worth investing your time and patience in your family.

The Tough Talks

Getting older means tackling more difficult things, like approaching your parents about some more serious issues. Maybe you need to ask them a very personal question, tell them about your first romance, admit you flunked a test, or caught your friend stealing and don't know what to do. Here are some suggestions on how to approach your parents when you want to have a meaningful, perhaps more difficult, conversation.

1. **Find the right time to talk.** Even though family is a priority, we are all busy and you want to find some uninterrupted time to approach your parent(s).

2. **Plan what you want to say.** Maybe even write it down to help you gather your thoughts. Also think about what your parents' responses might be.

3. **Stay calm** so you can think more clearly and articulate your thoughts more maturely.

4. **Be a good listener** when it's your parents' turn to talk. They may also need to think about what you have asked, so be courteous and give them time.

5. **Make a plan** to move forward and work together.

NEW ROMANCE

Experiencing romantic feelings for the first time is different for everyone. Most people have physical symptoms when they have this emotion. It can make your cheeks flush, make your heart race, or cause nervous butterflies in your stomach. For lack of better words, romance just makes you feel good inside. It's different than the feeling you have for your parent or your friend.

You may feel romantic about someone you have never even met, like a famous movie star or a singer. That is often referred to as having a crush on someone. You may daydream about that person or think about them more than usual. Sometimes existing friendships can change into crushes or romantic relationships. You often can't control who you have these feelings for, but you can decide if and how you want to react to your feelings. This takes courage.

There are many different ways to express your feelings. It can be as simple as talking to someone more than you used to or doing something nice for them that you wouldn't do for just any friend. Romantic relationships can become physical, including holding hands, hugging, kissing, or even having more physical affection. In today's world, a lot of romantic relationships involve more messaging using technology.

STAYING SAFE ON SOCIAL MEDIA

Social media allows you to constantly stay connected to your friends. When used properly, it can add to your sense of belonging. But many times, even with the best of intentions, social media can get people into predicaments that are difficult to navigate. It's important to know how to stay safe online and in the world of social media. Here are some guidelines.

★ Be careful with friend requests. Only "friend" people who you know IRL (in real life).

★ Maintain your privacy. Keep your settings set to private so you can control who is looking at you online.

★ Do not agree to meet someone IRL whom you have met only online.

★ Disable location services on your social media accounts.

★ Do not send naked pictures of your body. Do not ask others to send you a naked picture of themselves.

★ Alert a trusted adult if you aren't sure how to handle a situation or feel unsafe online.

And probably the most important thing of all:

Think before you post!

Having a romantic relationship should make you feel happy and feel good about yourself. But what if the person you feel attracted to doesn't feel the same way you do? Well . . . that is not uncommon and can make your heart hurt. Rejection is never easy. Although it may feel like it's the end of the world, there are many more opportunities down the road to discover new crushes and form new relationships.

Love is a big word and an intense feeling. There is no perfect or right definition of the word love, because your heart and mind are capable of loving many different people in many different ways. You likely love your family, your pets, and your friends. But romantic love is a different type of love, and the feelings can be intense.

Romantic love usually involves a physical connection—what most people call chemistry. It means two people are connected deeply to each other and committed to being there for each other. Opening yourself up to romantic relationships means that you are showing deep parts of yourself to someone else, and this can make you feel vulnerable. Romantic relationships, like friendships, can be long-lasting or can run their course until people begin to grow apart.

Of course, it's perfectly normal to be reading this and say to yourself, "Well, I don't have any romantic feelings right now!" These feelings develop over time. We don't have an exact age or timeline for romance. But we promise there is no reason to rush; it will happen when the time is right!

SEX AND SEXUALITY

· ·

The purpose of puberty, from the point of view of biology, is to get your body ready to make babies. How babies are made is an important topic that girls often have questions about. When a baby is made, that baby contains genetic material from a man and a woman—and what comes out is always unique. Here are the facts.

REPRODUCTION: THE FACTS

There are lots of fictitious tales about how babies come into this world. Maybe someone has told you that babies are delivered to the doorstep by a stork, fall from the sky, or get created from the birds and the bees. How you got created—and how any person became an actual living person in this world—involves a process called reproduction. Reproduction comes from the word reproduce, which means "to make again."

Understanding reproduction requires an understanding of male and female anatomy. Boys and girls have most of the same body parts. For example, we all have eyes, ears, hearts, lungs, and many more parts that help our bodies function. The differences between male and female bodies are your personal parts. Your personal parts, also called your private parts or genitals, are the parts that change during puberty. These parts are the ones that make reproduction possible.

Male Anatomy

You learned about female genitals in chapter 3. Now let's learn something about how boys are put together. To start, male genitals are mostly on the outside of their body.

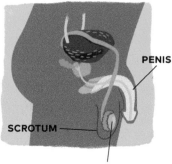

*   Penis: An organ hanging outside a man's body that is used for urinating, but also for transporting sperm out of a man's body.

*   Scrotum: A wrinkly sac of skin that sits underneath and on both sides of the penis. It's a carrying-case for the testicles.

*   Testicles: Two oval structures that sit inside the scrotum. These produce the sperm that will eventually travel to the penis.

Creating a baby requires a specific contribution from a man—the sperm—to meet with a specific contribution from a woman—the egg. This is done through a process called sexual intercourse, more commonly referred to as sex. The type of sex that is needed to make a baby requires that a man's penis goes inside of a woman's vagina. When it comes to reproduction, men and women fit together, like two pieces of a puzzle.

Sex and Pregnancy

So, here it is—the whole truth about sex. When two people have sex, a man's penis becomes hard (called an erection) as it prepares to enter the woman's vagina. During sex, semen, a fluid that contains sperm, leaves the man's body through his penis. This process is called ejaculation and is how the genes from a man get into a woman's body to mix with the genes in her egg to make a baby.

Inside a woman's body, another process is happening. If it's the right time in her menstrual cycle, a woman may have ovulated, or released an egg from her ovary. That egg begins to travel through the fallopian tube on its journey to the uterus. Meanwhile, the uterus has been busy building up a layer of blood inside of it to catch and nourish the egg. If the timing is exactly right, the sperm and the egg meet inside the fallopian tube and travel together to the uterus. They attach to the lining of the uterus. Once this happens, a woman is pregnant and a fetus begins to grow in her uterus.

Pregnancy is a long process—nine months long to be exact. Much has to be accomplished during this time. The fetus transforms from microscopic cells into a more recognizable baby, with internal organs, fingers, and toes. The blood-filled lining of the uterus, which is normally shed monthly during a woman's menstrual cycle, is kept inside the uterus during the entire pregnancy. Therefore, a woman has no periods during her pregnancy. This uterine lining turns into a new organ during pregnancy, called the placenta, which is how the fetus gets nourishment to grow.

After the nine months have passed and the baby is fully developed, it's ready to make its introduction into the world. The uterus, which is a giant muscle, has a final and very important job to do. It squeezes and contracts to help push the baby out of the woman's body at the end of pregnancy. There is only one natural way for the baby to get out, and that is through the stretchy tunnel connected to the uterus—the vagina.

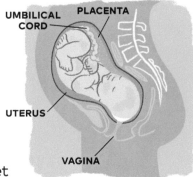

Often times girls have a lot of questions about sex and reproduction. We could write an entire book about this topic—but this is the short version of that science lesson! If you have more questions about sex and reproduction, there are resources in the back of the book you can talk about with your trusted adult.

Sex Without Pregnancy

It's important to know that people have sex for different reasons. Sometimes people have sex for the purpose of reproduction and to create a family. Sometimes people have sex just for enjoyment. Sex for reproduction must be between a man and a woman, but sex for pleasure can be between people of any gender identity and expression. If it's done in a loving and respectful manner, the act of sex is pleasurable. It's an intimate act that can feel good. While there is no exact age to start having sex, you should be a mature, consenting adult before making this decision.

Sex is the most personal act you can do with someone else; it's something that should be taken very seriously. You should only have sex with someone you feel comfortable, safe, and affectionate with.

SEX AND PORNOGRAPHY

Unfortunately, today's culture is full of misleading information and unhealthy portrayals of sex. Remember that things you may see online, on TV, or in movies are often not good examples of real sex.

Pornography (also known as porn) is videos and photographs that show sexual images intended to cause sexual arousal and curiosity. There are more pornography sites online than any other type of site on the Internet, so it can be easy to see inappropriate images without intentionally searching for them. If this happens to you, it's okay and normal to be curious. If you see images online that are inappropriate, don't be embarrassed or ashamed.

However, you should know that pornography is an unhealthy, unrealistic representation of what sex should be like. Thinking porn is real sex is like comparing fast racecar driving to driving in your neighborhood; it's not the same.

MASTURBATION

Masturbation is the act of touching yourself for pleasure. Masturbation is a way to explore your own body, including your private parts, in ways that make you feel good. Touching your genitals feels good in a different kind of way than touching your knee. There are many nerve endings in your genitals that make touching this area very pleasurable.

The most sensitive area of your genitals is a part called your clitoris. Your clitoris is located near the top of your vulva. It can vary in size; some clitorises are easy to see and some are not. Only a small part of the clitoris is on the outside of the body; most is hidden near the labia on either side of the opening to the vagina. It may become harder and easier to feel if you touch it. It's a very sensitive area of your body and touching it will make you feel good.

It's normal to masturbate and explore your body. Some people masturbate a lot, and some people never do. You should know that masturbation is not harmful to your body. Because masturbation involves touching your *private* parts, it's something you do in a *private* space, like your bedroom, without other people around. Masturbation is a normal way to get to know your own body and to explore your own sexuality.

PRIVACY AND CONSENT

Your body, and all of its parts, belong to YOU. Your body is private and you are in charge of it. Privacy and consent (giving permission) are important aspects of relationships with friends and family. They involve the use of good communication skills and respect. Honoring the rules of privacy and consent makes everyone more comfortable in a relationship.

Privacy

As you change physically and emotionally, you will likely desire more privacy. Your parents may not understand why you want your bedroom door closed more often, and you may not understand why your parents are so nosy and won't give you complete privacy. So as doctor moms, let us explain both sides of the story.

Your Side of the Story

As you start getting older, you will begin to value your alone time. You may need to take a break from your family from time to time and just want to chill out in your own space. That is perfectly normal. As doctors and moms, we know that you value your privacy and independence. Maybe there are conversations about your BFF's romance or your sibling's fight with a friend that you don't feel you want to share with your parents. What you decide is private is up to you, but remember, there are times when you may need an adult's advice on how to handle a situation. If there's a time where you are unsure about someone's safety, or if your intuition gives you an icky feeling that something is wrong, it's important to find a trusted adult to ask for help.

You may also start to want more physical privacy. As your body is changing, you may become more modest and not want to show your body to everyone. You may not want to keep the bathroom door open when you shower or change into your pajamas in front of your siblings or parents anymore. **Your body belongs to you and YOU make the rules for your body.**

Your Parents' Side of the Story

Your parents are adjusting to the independence you desire. They are used to knowing about everything going on with you, so it's hard for them to be left in the dark. Parents are often looking for signs that you are making good choices and can handle privacy responsibly. Your parents' biggest concern is always going to be your safety.

Technology is one area that your parents may decide to watch over closely, because there are many ways to get into trouble online. It's important to respect your parents' rules regarding technology because most likely they are paying the bills, so technically they can make the rules. Every family's rules are different. Your friends' parents may be very lax when it comes to rules about technology. Meanwhile, your parents may not let you be part of social media and may require the password to your phone. That is what your parents have decided is in your best interest. If you play by the rules and show you are responsible, you will likely earn more privileges over time.

Consent

Consent means giving permission. For you to consent to something, you need to clearly understand what it is you are agreeing to do. It's very important to understand and give consent when talking about your body. No one can touch your body without your specific permission.

You give consent often, even though you may not be thinking about it. When you reach out your hand to greet someone, you are actually giving consent for that person to touch your hand. When a friend asks to borrow your phone and you hand it over with a smile, you have given them consent to use your phone. Consent is most clear when it's given verbally, but there are other ways to convey your message.

Consent can be given in different ways.

* Verbal ("Yes! I am okay with that.")

* Body language (nodding your head, shaking a hand)

* Written (signing your name on an agreement or a permission slip)

When someone does not want to do something, there are often many clues in their body language. They may look downward, answer hesitantly or reluctantly, or change their tone of voice. But it's better to be direct so people don't have to guess about whether or not you are giving consent. When you clearly want to convey that you don't want to do something, looking someone in the eye and stating "no" clearly and firmly is the most effective way to communicate.

> Love yourself enough to set boundaries. . . . You teach people how to treat you by deciding what you will and won't accept.
>
> **–ANNA TAYLOR**

It Takes Two

Consent involves two people and must be mutual. Consent requires both people to feel comfortable with a situation. It's kind of like throwing a ball—you can't play catch on your own.

Here is an example:

You are shopping with your friend at the mall and find some cute shirts you want to try on. You go alone into the fitting room and close the door. A couple of different scenarios can unfold.

★ **Lack of communication.** Your friend opens the door so she can see the new shirt on you, but you are uncomfortable because you are half-naked and don't want her in there at that moment. This is a clear breach of your privacy and consent; she did not ask for your permission to enter.

★ **Clear consent.** Your friend knocks on the door, asks if she can come in, and you say, "Yes! I'd love your opinion on this shirt." That is clear consent to enter.

★ **Refusal of consent.** Your friend knocks on the door, asks if she can come in, and you say, "No! I'm not ready. I'll meet you outside when I'm done." That is clear that you do NOT give her consent to enter.

★ **Changing your mind.** Let's say you let your friend in to see the first shirt on you, but you still have more shirts to try on, so you close the door to the dressing room again. Just because you said "yes" once for her to enter the first time does NOT give her permission to peek in and see you in the other shirts, unless she asks again.

The same applies to anything that involves touching your body, whether it's holding hands, hugging, or having sex. You make the rules for your body—every single time.

What do you do if someone violates the rules of consent? Communicate! If it involves touching, you need to convey the message that you don't want to be touched, on that part, at that time. Anyone you allow to be that close to you should respect your wishes. If they don't, they are not respecting your boundaries. Pay attention to your intuition; it's there for a reason. If something doesn't feel right, then chances are it's not. You are allowed to tell that person loudly and clearly to STOP, and then talk about the situation with a trusted adult. It's your right to set your body boundaries.

THE WHOLE PICTURE

. . . .

You need to nurture your mind and body as it goes through all of the changes needed to become an adult. There are many things that can affect your physical health, but as doctors we also like to talk to our patients about their whole body wellness. There are four aspects to wellness.

- ★ Nutrition
- ★ Exercise
- ★ Sleep
- ★ Mood

These four things very strongly influence how your body feels. You may notice that they are also interconnected. For example, exercise can improve your mood and your sleep. Sleep influences your mood. The amount you exercise influences your nutrition, and vice versa. We like to think of these four things as the legs of a table: They are ALL necessary for you to feel well, and falling short on any one can make the table tip over.

Hopefully, you will begin to notice that the more you take care of your body, the more it takes care of you.

HEALTHY FOOD FOR A HEALTHY YOU

Nutrition and health go hand in hand. Taking care of your body means feeding yourself foods that nourish you. Your body is like a machine and the fuel we put in it matters. Fueling your body with foods that nourish you will keep your body feeling strong and healthy.

GOOD MOOD!
Nutrition Facts

Serving Size: 24 Hours

Regular Exercise   100%
Spend Time with Friends   100%
Get Enough Sleep   100%
Think Positive   100%
Eat Healthy   100%
Stay Hydrated   100%
Don't Let the Little Things Bother You 200%

There are many challenges to healthy eating. All around us there are restaurants, ice cream parlors, and treats. Often you may notice that it's difficult to make healthy choices if you are on the go. Making your nutrition a priority means that you have to plan your meals and be prepared. We understand that you are not always preparing your own food at home or at school, so do your best to make smart choices with what you are offered.

Here are some nutrition "Dos and Don'ts" to help you develop healthy habits:

Do:

* Eat whole foods (food from nature rather than processed in a machine)

* Make the first meal of your day a healthy one (include protein and healthy fat at breakfast to keep you full)

* Prepare most of your own food at home

* Snack mostly with foods from your refrigerator (think protein, fruits, and veggies)

* Eat only when you are hungry

* Ask yourself: How does this food make me feel after I eat it?

* Drink plenty of water (look for your urine to be light yellow or clear)

* Put snacks in a container to control the portion size

* Eat the rainbow (look for foods in a variety of colors)

Don't:

- ★ Eat mostly processed foods

- ★ Eat only snacks from your pantry

- ★ Eat when you are tired, thirsty, or bored

- ★ Drink beverages with sugar (like juice and soda)

- ★ Overeat (or eat until you feel uncomfortably full)

- ★ Eat quickly (you need to give your body time to send a signal to your brain that you are full)

Here are some tips to make healthy eating easier with your busy schedule.

- ★ Think about joining your parent at the grocery store. Not only will they love having you, but you can pick fresh, healthy food that you will be excited about for the week.

- ★ Cut up fruits and veggies in advance so there will be easy-to-grab, healthy snacks in your refrigerator, instead of always reaching in the pantry.

- ★ Help your parents with planning the dinner menu for the week. Try to pick at least three nights to eat in.

- ★ Keep a few of your favorite healthy snacks in a bag when you are doing activities away from home.

HEALTHY = BEAUTIFUL

Growing up means growing taller and getting curvier. It can be difficult to always be comfortable when your body is changing sizes. Your body's job is to grow and it needs proper nourishment to do that. You often hear about people going on diets to lose weight and change their body shape. While eating healthy is appropriate, eliminating any one food group or thinking about foods as "good" or "bad" can cause you to have unhealthy relationships with food.

Truth be told, we live in a society that focuses too much on body image. Our culture is obsessed with weight and pushes the idea that thinness equals beauty. But this is not true. Think about the women who inspire you. Do you look up to them just because of their body size? We hope not. Setting your sights on only being thin is problematic. Remember, magazine photos are airbrushed models and social media pictures are filtered, Photoshopped illusions. A *healthy* body is what we should all be working to achieve.

You can't eat "perfect" at every meal or every day, but you can try to develop good eating habits and increase your knowledge about healthy nutrition. You will find more information in the Resources section of this book.

> We get so worried about being pretty. Let's be pretty kind. Pretty funny. Pretty smart. Pretty strong.
>
> **–BRITT NICOLE**

MOVE YOUR BODY

Exercise benefits your body and your mind; everyone should get at least 60 minutes of exercise a day. The exercise should make your heart and lungs work harder and move faster. This may sound like another thing to add to your long list of to-dos, but anything that involves moving your body can be included in your 60 minutes. It doesn't have to be an organized sport or an expensive class at the nearby fitness center. You can achieve your exercise goal with gym class at school, walking around your block, meeting friends for a bike ride, or even just cranking up the music and dancing in your room.

Not all families are active or focus on their physical health. You may feel empowered by reading this to do things that benefit your health and then become a role model for your family and make exercise a family activity. The change can start with you.

Sixty minutes may sound like a lot of activity if you are currently inactive. You don't have to reach this goal overnight. Like any goal you want to achieve, it will take effort and perseverance. Set small, realistic goals and build up slowly. Start with a goal of a 10-minute walk around the block. As this becomes easier, you can increase the amount of time and effort until you reach your goal.

It's amazing that exercise:

* Improves your mood

* Helps you sleep better

* Makes your muscles and bones stronger

* Encourages other healthy habits

* Gives you the opportunity to meet new people

* Improves your confidence

Staying healthy involves effort, self-control, and motivation. You got this! You will never regret making yourself a priority.

BAD HABITS

There's a lot of positive growth that happens in adolescence, but of course, there are always dangers that your newfound independence can expose you to. When you are a teen, you will establish many new habits, and these can include bad habits. These bad habits are particularly dangerous for teens because your brain is still undergoing a process of development (see chapter 5). This makes your teen brain more likely to take dangerous risks without thinking about the consequences.

Examples of bad habits include:

* Smoking cigarettes

* Vaping and Juuling

* Drinking alcohol

* Using other people's prescription medications (like opiates, benzodiazepines, or stimulants)

* Smoking marijuana

* Trying illegal drugs

These chemicals negatively affect your body, including your heart and lungs. They also disrupt your self-control, memory, concentration, learning, attention, and mood. Your body and brain are still growing and developing, and are at increased risk of damage from experimenting with these substances. Your brain is also more susceptible to becoming addicted to substances.

When confronted with a choice, take an extra second to pause and ask yourself, "Do I *really* want to do this?" and "Do I think this is the *right* thing to do?" Life is full of choices, and there will be times when the choices you make are not the best ones. Adolescence is about learning from your mistakes, so that you can reach adulthood happy and healthy.

SLEEP

Sleep is one of the healthiest things you can do for your body. Sleep influences your moods and behavior, your attention, and your physical health. Never underestimate the importance of getting enough sleep. Without it, puberty can be much more difficult.

While you sleep, your body and mind repair themselves. What happens to a light when it's not turned off? It eventually burns out. The same happens to your energy, your patience, and your skills if you don't give your body and brain time to rest. Sleep is the most important medicine you can give your body to keep it functioning well.

How much sleep is enough? On average, you should be getting nine hours of sleep per night. This is what your body needs during puberty to run a healthy machine. Do you find you are getting less sleep than that? That's common, for a variety of reasons:

★ **You are busy.** Older kids often have activities later at night and more homework to do.

★ **Your internal clock changed time zones.** One of the hallmarks of becoming a teenager is your ability to stay up later and sleep in later. Your circadian rhythm, which is your built-in body clock, is changing. Melatonin (sleep hormone) gets released later at night and shifts your sleeping pattern.

★ **Technology.** Cell phones and electronics interfere with going to bed on time and interrupt sleep.

★ **Your brain.** Mood issues can cause you to be more tired or can make it difficult to fall asleep.

COOL AND CONFIDENT

When you feel better physically, you feel better mentally. Good nutrition and exercise can improve your self-confidence. Healthy habits give you more positive energy to take on life's challenges and enjoy your activities. Your body physically becomes stronger; it gives you an amazing feeling of what you can physically accomplish when you see what your body can lift and how far it can run. Don't forget to celebrate your accomplishments and reflect on how strong you are. You can celebrate the small victories, like making it through a tough day, and the big victories, like completing a race.

Good Sleep Hygiene

Sleep hygiene refers to the habits you create to allow yourself to sleep well. Here are some of the cornerstones of good sleep hygiene.

Tips to HELP you sleep:

★ Go to bed at the same time each day.

★ Get regular exercise each day, preferably in the morning. There is good evidence that regular exercise improves restful sleep.

★ Keep your bedroom quiet, dark, and cool for the best sleep environment.

* Use your bed only for sleep (not for homework or using electronics).

* Charge your electronics elsewhere and don't sleep with them in your room.

* Use a relaxation exercise just before going to sleep (such as muscle relaxation, guided imagery, self-massage, taking a warm bath or shower, deep breathing, etc.).

Things that INTERFERE with sleep:

* Exercising just before going to bed.

* Having caffeine in the evening (coffee, tea, chocolate, some sodas).

* Using technology in bed or watching TV in bed. The light affects your melatonin (sleep hormone) and your ability to fall asleep.

* Going to bed too hungry or too full.

* Taking daytime naps longer than 15 to 30 minutes.

* Using your phone as an alarm clock (charge your phone in the kitchen!).

Sleep is the glue that holds you together. Make it a priority to have good sleep habits.

MOOD

We have talked in detail about moods in chapter 5, but it's important to remember that your mood can affect your physical wellness. Science has proven the link between mental health and physical health. For example, if you have chronic stress, your body may respond by giving you stomachaches or high blood pressure. If you are happy and grateful, you have a better immune system and less heart disease. The mind–body connection is fascinating!

Also remember, mood swings are going to happen. You can be mad and frustrated one minute and full of joy and laughter the next. Having the full range of emotions is not unique to being a teen—it means that you are *human*. Think about your feelings like waves in the ocean: They crash on the shore and they roll back out again. Both actions are part of a powerful natural cycle.

A FINAL WORD

Congratulations on taking the time to learn about this special time in your life! You should celebrate your transition into adolescence and be proud of the person you are becoming. During puberty there is a lot happening to you, and you can't be an expert in everything, so don't be afraid to ask questions. The more you understand about your changing body, the more you will respect your amazing self.

You are capable and prepared to tackle adolescence and the joys and challenges it brings. Life will always have ups and downs, but by reading this book and continuing to learn about your body and brain, you will have the knowledge to tackle anything that comes your way. Surround yourself with a winning team that supports you for who you want to be.

LOVE YOURSELF. IT'S TRENDING.

RESOURCES FOR YOU

‖ ‖

BOOKS FOR YOU TO CHECK OUT

Covey, Sean. *The 7 Habits of Highly Effective Teens.* New York: Touchstone, 2014.
This book offers a series of steps to follow to help teach teens how to become confident, self-sufficient, and successful in whatever path they choose.

Harris, Robie. *It's So Amazing: A Book About Eggs, Sperm, Birth, Babies, and Families.* Somerville, Massachusetts: Candlewick Press, 2014.
An illustrated book with honest answers about reproduction, having babies, sex, and sexuality.

Harris, Robie. *It's Perfectly Normal: Changing Bodies, Growing Up, Sex, and Sexual Health.* Somerville, Massachusetts: Candlewick Press, 2009.
An illustrated book about puberty, reproduction, and sexuality.

Metzger, Julie. *Will Puberty Last My Whole Life? Real Questions from Preteens About Body Changes, Sex, and Other Growing-Up Stuff.* Seattle: Little Bigfoot, 2012.
A puberty books about girls and boys, in question-and-answer format.

Silverberg, Cory. *Sex Is a Funny Word: A Book About Bodies, Feelings, and YOU.* New York: Triangle Square, 2015.
A sex education book that is inclusive of lesbian, gay, and bisexual experiences as well as gender creative and gender nonconforming children.

WEBSITES FOR YOU TO CHECK OUT

Amaze

amaze.org
AMAZE takes the awkward out of sex ed. Real info in fun, animated videos that give you all the answers you actually want to know about sex, your body, and relationships.

A Mighty Girl

amightygirl.com
A huge collection of books, toys, and movies for smart, confident, and courageous girls.

Bedsider

bedsider.org
Information on birth control.

Environmental Working Group Skin Deep Guide

ewg.org/skindeep/

Guide for safe skin products to protect yourself and your family from chemicals.

Girlshealth

girlshealth.gov

Provides girls with reliable information on hundreds of topics related to health and well-being.

Go Ask Alice!

goaskalice.columbia.edu

A website from Columbia University that answers questions about your health that may be difficult to ask adults.

Healthy Children

healthychildren.org

Information from the American Academy of Pediatrics, which is dedicated to providing resources on the health, safety, and well-being of infants, children, adolescents, and young adults.

Kids Health

kidshealth.org

Kids Health is a nonprofit organization to help kids, teens, and parents take care of their health.

U by Kotex

ubykotex.com

Products to help take care of your period and videos to help you learn all about your period.

She Lift

shelift.org

SheLift is a nonprofit organization that empowers young women and girls with physical differences to discover confidence and self-esteem through outdoor recreation and mentorship.

Tampax

tampax.com

Products to help take care of your period and information to help you learn all about your period.

Thinx Period Underwear

shethinx.com

Thinx washable underwear can be worn during menstruation as an alternative to traditional feminine hygiene products.

Turning Teen

turningteen.com

Turning Teen provides educational programs created by two pediatricians to start the conversation with parents and children about their bodies.

MENTAL AND EMOTIONAL HEALTH RESOURCES FOR YOU

If you need to just talk to someone:

★   Call Teen Line at 1-800-TLC-TEEN

★   Text 'TEEN' to 839863

★   Visit https://teenlineonline.org/talk-now

If you are in crisis or have thoughts about hurting yourself:

★ Call the National Suicide Prevention Lifeline at 1-800-273-TALK (8255)

★ Text the Crisis Text Line by texting 'TALK' to 741741

★ http://www.afsp.org (American Foundation for Suicide Prevention)

If someone else is hurting you or you are unsafe in your home:

★ Call the National Domestic Violence Hotline at 1-800-799-7233

★ http://www.ndvh.org

APPS FOR YOUR TECHNOLOGY

Calm

calm.com
Guided meditations to help you practice mindfulness, manage anxiety, lower stress, and sleep better.

Clue

helloclue.com
Track your period and ovulation schedule.

Headspace

headspace.com
Teaches meditation and mindfulness to help you relax and sleep better.

Period Tracker

gpapps.com

Track your periods and predict when they are coming next.

Teen Hotlines

apps.apple.com/us/app/teen-hotlines/id427614056

Lists hotlines, help lines, and websites organized by subject. From school violence and depression to eating disorders and suicide, these national organizations can also refer you to state, provincial, and local services in your community.

ThinkUp

thinkup.me

Positive affirmations and daily motivation so you can develop the mind-set and motivation you need to succeed.

Waterlogged

waterlogged.com

It'll track your water consumption to see how you're doing during the day, plus you can snap pics of your own glasses to log even faster. And you can set it to remind you when to stop what you're doing and take a sip.

RESOURCES AND SUGGESTED READING FOR ADULTS

BOOKS FOR ADULTS

Damour, Lisa. *Untangled: Guiding Teenage Girls Through the Seven Transitions into Adulthood*. New York: Ballantine Books, 2016.

Damour, Lisa. *Under Pressure: Confronting the Epidemic of Stress and Anxiety in Girls*. New York: Ballantine Books, 2019.

Greenspan, Louise, and Julianna Deardorff. *The New Puberty: How to Navigate Early Development in Today's Girls*. Emmaus, Pennsylvania: Rodale Books, 2015.

Jensen, Frances E., and Amy Ellis Nutt. *The Teenage Brain. A Neuroscientist's Survival Guide to Raising Adolescents and Young Adults*. New York: HarperCollins, 2016.

Jenson, Kristen. *Good Pictures. Bad Pictures. Porn-Proofing Today's Young Kids*. Glen Cove, New York: Glen Cove Press, 2018.

Kliegman, Robert M., MD, Bonita Stanton, MD, Joseph St. Geme, MD, and Nina F. Schor, MD, PhD. *Nelson's Textbook of Pediatrics*. New York: Elsevier, 2015.

Siegel, Daniel J. *Brainstorm: The Power and Purpose of the Teenage Brain*. Vancouver, British Columbia: Langara College, 2017.

Simmons, Rachel. *Enough as She Is: How to Help Girls Move Beyond Impossible Standards of Success to Live Healthy, Happy, and Fulfilling Lives*. New York: Harper, 2019.

Wiseman, Rosalind. *Queen Bees and Wannabes: Helping Your Daughter Survive Cliques, Gossip, Boyfriends, and Other Realities of Adolescence*. New York: Three Rivers Press, 2002.

ONLINE RESOURCES FOR ADULTS

American Academy of Pediatrics

AAP.org

The members of the American Academy of Pediatrics include board-certified pediatricians who dedicate their efforts and resources to the health, safety, and well-being of infants, children, adolescents, and young adults.

American College of Obstetrics and Gynecology

ACOG.org

A professional organization and governing body of physicians specializing in obstetrics and gynecology.

Common Sense Media

commonsensemedia.org

A nonprofit organization that promotes safe technology and media for children.

Environmental Working Group

ewg.org

A nonprofit organization that specializes in research and advocacy in the areas of agricultural subsidies, toxic chemicals, drinking water pollutants, and corporate accountability.

Gender Spectrum

genderspectrum.org

Gender Spectrum helps to create gender-sensitive and inclusive environments for all children and teens.

Sex Positive Families

sexpositivefamilies.com

An organization focused on strengthening sexual health and body awareness talks between parents and children through education, resources, and supportive services.

Society for Adolescent Health and Medicine

adolescenthealth.org

A multidisciplinary organization committed to improving the physical and psychosocial health and well-being of adolescents and young adults through advocacy, clinical care, health promotion, professional development, and research.

Trans Student Educational Resources

transstudent.org/gender

Trans Student Educational Resources is a youth-led organization dedicated to transforming the educational environment for trans and gender nonconforming students through advocacy and empowerment.

REFERENCES

Ackerman, Courtney. "What Is Self-Esteem? A Psychologist Explains." PositivePsychology.com. May 5, 2018. https://positivepsychology.com/self-esteem/.

Biro, Frank, MD, and Yee-Ming Chan, MD, PhD. "Normal Puberty." UpToDate. July 2018. https://www.uptodate.com/contents/normal-puberty.

Brown, Dana. "Why Talking About Teen Body Image Is as Important as the 'Sex Talk.'" The MD.com Blog. June 6, 2018. https://www.md.com/blog/talking-about-teen-body-image-as-important-as-the-sex-talk.

Carter, Christine. "Three Ways to Help Out Your Stressed-Out Teenager." Mindful. May 13, 2019. https://www.mindful.org/three-ways-to-help-your-stressed-out-teenager/.

Castle, Jill. "Teenage Weight Gain (What You Can Do)." August 8, 2018. https://jillcastle.com/teenager-nutrition/teenage-weight-gain-what-to-do/.

Damour, Lisa. "Teenagers Do Dumb Things, but There Are Ways to Limit Recklessness." *New York Times*. March 8, 2017. https://www.nytimes.com/2017/03/08/well/family /teenagers-do-dumb-things-but-there-are-ways-to-limit -recklessness.html.

Ellsworth, Belinda. "The Difference Between Self-Confidence and Self-Esteem." Step Into Success. April 15, 2017. https ://www.stepintosuccess.com/difference-self-confidence -self-esteem/.

Girls Inc. "Tips for Answering Your Child's Questions About Sexuality." June 2017. https://girlsinc.org/app/uploads /2017/06/Tips-for-Answering-Your-Child's-Questions- About-Sexuality.pdf.

Gordon, Hilary, MD. "Vaping: What You Need to Know." Teens Health, February 2019. https://kidshealth.org/en /teens/e-cigarettes.html.

Harvard Graduate School of Education. "5 Tips for Guiding Teens and Young Adults in Developing Healthy Romantic Relationships." Making Caring Common Project. October 2018. https://mcc.gse.harvard.edu/resources-for-families/5-tips -parents-guiding-teens-healthy-romantic-relationships.

The Harvard Health Blog. "The Adolescent Brain: Beyond Raging Hormones." March 2011. https://www.health.harvard .edu/mind-and-mood/the-adolescent-brain-beyond-raging -hormones.

Jacobsen, Maryann, MS, RD. "13 Things Girls with a Healthy Body Image Don't Do (And How Parents Help Them)." May 23, 2019. https://maryannjacobsen.com/healthy-body-image -girls/?fbclid=IwAR2ARSMe73d9zqyBb8TF1chGfMvlKAyUISZjC HyyEfiUbbCFHr-CrIv-bxs.

Macmillan, Amanda. "Why Instagram Is the Worst Social Media for Mental Health." *Time*. May 25, 2017. http://time .com/4793331/instagram-social-media-mental-health/.

Office of Disease Prevention and Health Promotion. "Dietary Guidelines for Americans, 2015–2020." https://health.gov /dietaryguidelines/2015/guidelines/.

Pfarrer, Steve. "Perfection Is Not a Solution: Rachel Simmons Looks for Ways for Young Women to Find Balance in Their Lives." Amherst Bulletin. February 22, 2018. https://www. amherstbulletin.com/Making-girls-confident-Smith-College -development-specialist-pens-new-book-15214118.

Ross, Franzi. "Stress vs. Anxiety—Knowing the Difference Is Critical to Your Health." Mental Health First Aid Blog. June 8, 2018. https://www.mentalhealthfirstaid.org/external/2018 /06/stress-vs-anxiety/.

Sex Info Online. "An Overview of Sex and Sexuality." February 22, 2018. https://sexinfo.soc.ucsb.edu/article/overview-sex -and-sexuality.

Silverman, Robyn, MD. "How to Ensure That Every Girl Knows She Is Enough as She Is, with Rachel Simmons." Dr. Robyn (Podcast). https://drrobynsilverman.com/how-to-ensure-that-every-girl-knows-she-is-enough-as-she-is-with-rachel-simmons/.

Simmons, Rachel. "How to Raise a Confident Daughter in a Toxic Culture." March 7, 2018. https://www.rachelsimmons.com/how-to-raise-a-confident-daughter-in-a-toxic-culture/.

INDEX

ACKNOWLEDGMENTS

This book, and our company, Turning Teen, is a labor of love. We feel passionate about educating parents and kids about topics related to adolescence. It has been an honor (and a wonderful challenge!) to write this book and put our thoughts down on paper.

This book would not have been possible without the help of some very important people.

First and foremost, we thank our families for believing in us and always being our biggest cheerleaders. Thank you to our husbands, who give us time to pursue our passion projects. We are grateful to our children, who give us endless experience, credibility, and challenges that make us better. We know that parenting is our most difficult yet most rewarding work.

Thank you to all of the families who have participated in Turning Teen. Your enthusiasm for our work and countless questions provide us with the fuel we need to continue this passion. Last, thank you to Callisto Media for their support and collaboration on this project.

ABOUT THE AUTHORS

Credit: Christine Long

DR. LISA KLEIN practices pediatrics in Michigan. She stays busy with her three boys (two sons and one husband!). Dr. Lisa's passion for teaching adolescents and parents how to communicate and have those not-so-comfortable talks together has inspired her practice and shaped her career. In between work, kids' activities, and volunteering as a summer camp doctor, she constantly seeks ways to continue learning and to help ensure kids are healthy and happy in the communities she serves.

Credit: Christine Long

DR. CARRIE LEFF practices internal medicine and pediatrics in Michigan. She is passionate about all aspects of women's health. Her passion led her to Turning Teen, where she enjoys educating and helping kids and parents navigate the perils and pitfalls of puberty. As the mother of three daughters, Dr. Carrie truly understands the pressures that both teens and their parents face during adolescence. She considers motherhood to be her greatest challenge and reward.

Dr. Lisa and Dr. Carrie first crossed paths as friends and colleagues during their residencies at William Beaumont Hospital in Michigan. Their shared passion for adolescent health, puberty talks, and art projects spurred a revolutionary idea to fill a need in their communities. Together they created and launched Turning Teen, a business designed to help tweens transition into adolescence without shame, secrecy, or embarrassment. They bring puberty educational workshops to comfortable spaces and open the dialogue about changing bodies between tweens, teens, and trusted adults. Turning Teen presents small groups, clubs, and full auditoriums with the information needed to start the conversation.